Endorsements

Loosed to Love takes women beyond survival from past pain into the discovery of the purpose that awaits them in the presence of God. Evangelist Rita Twiggs has a unique gift to lead women beyond the cold, calloused heart of brokenness into the warm embrace of an intimate relationship with God. This is a must for women who are ready to take the next step. I think men would be blessed by it as well. Go on, pick it up, and be transformed while you read!

BISHOP T. D. JAKES, SR.
Author of *Woman, Thou Art Loosed*
Senior Pastor, The Potter's House, Dallas, Texas

Loosed to Love is wonderfully enjoyable writing! Dr. Rita Twiggs vividly shares about her "romance" with the Father. Her stories are endearing and coupled with powerful principles to learn. I highly recommend this book. It will set you on a path of pursuit to experience intimacy with God as never before imagined!

DR. KINGSLEY A. FLETCHER
Senior Pastor, Life Community Church
Research Triangle Park, North Carolina

Endorsements

Once you start to read this book, you will have a difficult time putting it down. Dr. Twiggs has given us a real-life testimony of finding the Lover of her soul. Once you find Him, there's no way you'll ever be the same or let Him go! As you read about her experience, you will start to assess your "knowing" of Him. When you begin to identify with God, your relationship with Him will begin to adjust, renew, and be made more precious. You too will be *Loosed to Love.*

BISHOP RALPH L. DENNIS
Presiding Bishop
Kingdom Fellowship Covenant Ministries

Evangelist Twiggs has illuminated the Bible principle "first natural, then spiritual." She makes her life a living tutorial for the seeker or the seasoned saint who is serious about intimacy with God. You will smile and maybe blush a bit; then you will get the point! Read it, and get ready for His embrace!

REV. DR. CLAUDETTE ANDERSON COPELAND
New Creation Christian Fellowship
San Antonio, Texas

Endorsements

What an awesome, bold declaration Dr. Rita Twiggs' new book, *Loosed to Love,* shares!

Dr. Twiggs' book is a true "portrait of intimacy" as she pours out her heart in personal experiences that become biblical tools. She reminds all of us that while we search for "flesh and blood" to provide intimate relations in our lives, God Himself has been *waiting* for, *working* with, *watching* over, and *wooing* us all the time. In other words, He has been wanting to love us, to be there with and for us...all the time.

Thank you, Dr. Twiggs, for reminding me personally that there is a part of my heart, soul, and mind that belongs only to God. There is that special part of me that can be filled wholly by the Lord Jesus Christ. No man, woman, boy, or girl can relate to me as God can. Too often, we have forgotten this truth, and when we do, we can end up angry, uptight, and frustrated.

Dr. Twiggs' book releases us to enjoy the love of God. We can no longer blame parents, spouses, friends, and associates for that for which they are not responsible. This book released me to enjoy life planned for me by God before the foundation of the world. When we enter into God's purposes for us, then, and only then, can we know true peace, true love, and true rest.

Thanks, Lady Rita!

DR. WANDA A. TURNER
Best-selling author, speaker, associate pastor

LOOSED
TO
LOVE

LOOSED TO LOVE

Dr. Rita Twiggs

Whitaker House

Unless otherwise indicated, Scripture quotations are taken from the *New King James Version*, © 1979, 1980, 1982 by Thomas Nelson, Inc. Used by permission. All rights reserved.

Scripture quotations marked (KJV) are taken from the *King James Version* of the Bible.

Scripture quotations marked (NIV) are from the Holy Bible, *New International Version*, © 1973, 1978, 1984 by the International Bible Society. Used by permission.

LOOSED TO LOVE

Rita Twiggs Ministries, Inc.
P.O. Box 64223
Washington, DC 20029
www.rltministries.org

ISBN: 0-88368-651-1
Printed in the United States of America
Copyright © 2000 by Rita L. Twiggs

Whitaker House
30 Hunt Valley Circle
New Kensington, PA 15068

Library of Congress Cataloging-in-Publication Data

Twiggs, Rita L., 1951–
     Loosed to love : a portrait of intimacy / by Rita L. Twiggs.
       p. cm.
     ISBN 0-88368-651-1 (pbk. : alk. paper)
     1. God—Worship and love. 2. Twiggs, Rita L., 1951– I. Title.
     BV4817 .T95 2001
     248.2–dc21
                                              00-012770

1 2 3 4 5 6 7 8 9 10 11 12 13/ 09 08 07 06 05 04 03 02 01 00

Dedication

This book is dedicated to all my loved ones,
especially Jesus, the Lover of my soul.

Contents

Foreword...13

PART I: LOOSED FROM BONDAGE

My Story...17

1. Freedom from Bondage 19

2. The Lover of My Soul 33

PART II: LOOSED TO LOVE JESUS

Embracing Him 45

3. I Really Do Want to Satisfy Him...................47

4. He Can Be Trusted 61

PART III: LOOSED FOR TRUE WORSHIP

Pathway to Intimacy...75

The Pattern of Worship

5. The Outer Court and the Holy Place 77

6. Entering the Holy of Holies 97

The Posture of Worship

7. Anointing the Lord 115

8. Breaking the Alabaster Box 129

The Perfection of Worship

9. Glory in Unity...145

PART IV: LOOSED FOR PURPOSE

An Overflow of Divine Life................................163

10. Walk Right into It 165

11. The Secret Ingredient 183

12. Handfuls of Purpose 191

13. Stay on the Pathway..................................205

Epilogue..215

About the Author 219

Foreword

I have lived almost half a century, and I have never understood real intimacy until now. I've had my share of relationships, both good and bad; but the one I'm about to share with you has no equal. Normally, because I am a very private person, I wouldn't think of exposing my feelings and experiences in print. However, in response to Holy pressure, I have penned these pages with the prayer that you, the reader, might be blessed to share my testimony as one who has been *Loosed to Love!*

Throughout this book, you will find that I use the language of love and intimacy in a very straightforward way. I have done so because I have come to have a love relationship with Jesus that is so deep that only such terms of intimacy can adequately describe it. I also think that it will enable you to better understand what I'm trying to communicate and teach about having an intimate relationship with Jesus. He desires to have such a relationship with all who belong to His church as the bride of Christ. My prayer is that you will come to understand the close communion that you also can have with Jesus your Bridegroom, the Lover of your soul.

As I was working on this book, there was a little voice sitting on my left shoulder, saying, "Don't finish this book. What you're describing sounds too much like the worldly kind of love. It has too much 'mushy' stuff in it." However, there was another voice sitting on my right shoulder, saying that many who read this book will take another look at Jesus and will embark upon the journey of a lifetime as they seek a new level of intimacy with Him. Still others who have never known real love will be thrust onto the pathway of intimacy and discover for the first time the true Lover of their souls, Jesus.

This is the pathway of freedom and true worship, which will lead to joyful service and love toward God and others!

PART I
Loosed from Bondage

Loosed from Bondage

My Story

There are many things in life that can make us feel unloved, unfulfilled, and destined to failure. They bind us so that, although we struggle against them, we find it hard to rise above them and find freedom. Because we're in the midst of a frustrating struggle, we miss out on what is most important in life—being loved by a God who loves us with all of His heart, and loving Him back with all of our hearts in indescribable freedom and joy.

That was my story. But I have a new story to tell. This book tells how I found freedom from bondage, learned to love the Lover of my soul, and discovered a joyful life fulfilling the purposes of God. Come with me as I tell you about my journey, and join me on the pathway to intimacy. At the first stop on the journey, you will find...

...Freedom from Bondage

Chapter One

Freedom from Bondage

At first it seemed surreal, like a dream. I was working for a national ministry, and traveling all over the country to one conference after another. My job was to make the announcements, lead worship, and do the introductions. I found myself introducing big-name celebrities and brushing shoulders with stars. All of a sudden, I was meeting heroes I had heretofore only admired from afar. I got the chance to ride in a beautiful stretch limousine—with Vicki Winans, no less, who is a wonderful and witty woman. On another occasion, when I found out I was sitting next to Marvin Winans, I could have fainted. And one night, I even chitchatted on stage with Shirley Caesar. Did you hear that? I said *the* Shirley Caesar.

Now, if that wasn't enough, when I, little ole me, actually handed Donnie McClurkin the microphone, I vowed I'd never wash my hand again. I felt as though I had been translated from one place and time into a field of dreams. But even with all this apparent fulfillment and success, I didn't have complete peace. Underlying fears and insecurities quietly gnawed at me. Little did I know then that my coming to work for this ministry was all a big setup, orchestrated by the Lover of my soul. The One who died and rose again two thousand years ago, the same One who had saved me as a little girl, was now orchestrating a deeper dimension of salvation for me as a woman.

The Bondage of Fear

Oh, I was saved and on my way to heaven; I was following the Lord and trying to understand and walk in His purposes for me; but for years I had been locked in a world of fear and intimidation. Many fears had gripped my soul. Some were telling me not to try because I would fail; others were saying not to risk loving because I'd get hurt. These fears were robbing me of the love relationship with Christ that I was meant to have and the fullness of ministry He desired for me. Have you ever felt such fears? They're paralyzing, aren't they?

Fear is one of the deadliest bondages. Let me tell you why I say that. The Bible makes reference to fear, its torment, and its treatment, over 365 times, because it is so destructive. Fear is like a silent disease that sneaks in unawares; if it is not diagnosed and treated early, it will devastate even the strongest person. Fear is so subtle that you can stumble because of it and not even see that it is there. It feels like an emotion, but the Bible calls it a "spirit." Second Timothy 1:7 says, *"For God has not given us a spirit of fear, but of power and of love and of a sound mind,"* and Romans 8:15 says, *"For you did not receive the spirit of bondage again to fear, but you received the Spirit of adoption by whom we cry out, 'Abba, Father.'"*

> Fear must be evicted by the Holy Spirit's perfect love in order for true deliverance to take place.

Maybe that's why fear is so strong! As a spirit, fear invades the human spirit, and it must be evicted by the perfect love of the Holy Spirit in order for true deliverance to take place. I'm going to repeat that statement because it's so important: fear must be evicted by the perfect love of the Holy Spirit in order for true deliverance to take place.

Fear can latch onto any life situation that comes our way, and invade our spirits before we know it. It acts like a poisonous snakebite that releases venom into the bloodstream and makes its way to the heart. The Word of God says, *"For as he thinks in his heart, so is he"* (Proverbs 23:7). Now, when our hearts are full of fear, we are paralyzed by its venom, and all of our faculties are deadened. We are left incapacitated and unable to function. If an antidote is not soon administered, fear can destroy us spiritually, emotionally, mentally, and even financially. And that's not all. As fear destroys us, it can use us to destroy others, thereby making it a threat to families, communities, and even a whole nation.

Fear is cruel. It knows no age, color, or gender. But in my battles with fear, God has constantly been there with me and has shown me the way out. I want to share some of these experiences with you now, with the prayer that they will help you to realize that you, too, can be free from the bondage of fear or any other bondages that you might be facing.

As a child, I can remember nights when I would have bad dreams and go running to my mother's room for comfort, or be frozen in fear and scream for help. Thank God for a mother who never laughed at me or fussed at me in my fear. She took it seriously, and prayed or sang or read to me until I drifted peacefully off to sleep again. I believe that mothers and fathers should do this for their children, to help free them from their fears.

I also remember a time when my sisters and I had to go to the day nursery because our mother, who was a single parent, had to work. I wasn't old enough to watch my siblings at home. There was a mean-hearted old woman at the nursery who would beat my sister for no apparent reason. (We didn't know about child protective services then.) Almost every day, she would find a reason to beat my sister, and every day, I found myself filled with two fears: fear of what she was doing to my sister, and fear of what I wanted to do to her. Even at a young age, I was afraid that if I *ever* got the chance, I'd...well, you know!

Surely, I thank God for the birthdays that passed quickly, until the day came when we no longer had to go to the nursery. I can see how the grace and mercy of God kept me and calmed my fears until deliverance came—just in time.

Fear Subsides—for a While

As I got older, I experienced different types of fears. At first, I was afraid that my classmates would not like me—and some of them didn't. Many liked me, however, and I learned that everyone did not have to like me for me to be happy. I just needed to like myself and treat others right. God gave me this understanding in order to deliver me from my fear of being rejected.

Then I was afraid that my teacher would call on me to solve a problem I didn't really understand—and she did. I ended up learning so much from this teacher, who challenged me to try, even though I was afraid. In addition, my awesome mother would constantly remind me that I could do anything I set my mind to, with God's help! Armed with this assurance, I tackled task after task in junior and senior high school, and my fears subsided for quite a while. I was not afraid to audition as the youngest member of the high school band. When my mother married a captain in the U.S. Air Force, and I changed schools as an "Air Force brat," I was not afraid to make new friends and try new things like mountain camping. I even convinced myself that, with God's help, I could be the first female and the first African-American to be student conductor in a recently integrated school. I auditioned with no fear, and when I won this post, I conducted the concert band in the same way.

In the same fearless manner, I flew alone halfway around the world to launch out on my own at the age of nineteen. I went to school by day, worked until midnight, and caught the bus home at night alone. I can recall only one instance when fear resurfaced. That was the night that two men robbed me a block from my home. Ironically, I did not become afraid until after I had chased them with my umbrella and run to the police precinct to report the incident. Then, as I recounted to the officer what had happened, fear of what *could* have happened to me gripped my soul. I remember falling asleep thanking God for keeping me alive in the midst of my foolishness. The next morning, the fear was gone!

Later, as I entered into ministry, I was not afraid to answer God's call, although I had obstacles to overcome. I had grown up in a traditional church community that believed women were to be seen but not heard. The brothers were kind to me as a sister, but they were constantly expressing their belief that women shouldn't preach or teach. Strangely enough, they believed a woman could witness, pray, and lay hands on the sick for healing. But preach? That seemed to be reserved for their elite club, and to my surprise, many times the sisters were in total agreement with them.

> Worshipers have the secret weapon of prayer and praise.

If I hadn't known that I was called of God to preach, I would have been most miserable. However, even with the assurance of God's calling, it was very frustrating to have to press beyond the double standard that had been set. Fortunately, I was a worshiper, and worshipers have the secret weapon of prayer and praise. This was a real blessing to me because, through prayer and praise, God dried my tears. Through prayer and praise, God strengthened my faith. Through prayer and praise, I received grace that was sufficient to overcome persecution, prejudice, and rejection, no matter what the source.

For years I traveled alone to cities, states, and countries without fear. I did not fear standing to teach or preach because I had prayed to God when He first called me and asked Him to give me somewhere to preach, something to preach, and not to let me preach error. He answered so well that I never had to ask anyone to let me preach; He always gave me a message to preach, and He always helped me to preach truth without fear—with or without the approval of others.

A New Fear Surfaces

Then, one day, seemingly without warning, at the age of forty, a new kind of fear crept into my spirit. Perhaps it began with the sting of failing to finish my degree along with my class. Maybe it took root and spread during the dawn of the computer revolution when I began to feel inadequate in my ability to master the latest technology. All I know is that one day I was full of confidence, and seemingly overnight, I woke up to find myself tormented by a cruel *fear of failure*. I emphasize this particular fear because, even though there have been many types of fears in my life, this is the one that poisoned my system and ate away at the very fiber of who I was.

I allowed other people to define my self-worth. That was a big mistake! You see, while many loving people poured encouragement into my soul, many others dumped buckets of mockery and belittlement into me. These doused my self-esteem with waters of degrading thoughts. Consequently, these thoughts haunted me until negative self-talk and self-abasement ruled my mind.

I devoted my life to being a people pleaser. By the term *people pleaser,* I mean that I was constantly struggling to make other people happy, no matter what the cost to me. I would buy things to be accepted, only to see others accept the things, but not me. I would say yes when I really wanted to say no, which only caused me to lose my self-respect more and more. I would back down, even when I knew I was right, so as not to be rejected—only to be rejected anyway. The harder I tried, the more I realized that I was pleasing some of the people some of the time, a few of the people most of the time, and none of the people all of the time—while pleasing God hardly any of the time.

Little did I know then that God was jealous over me and my time, and that He doesn't play second fiddle! He wanted me to please Him first. If I did that, then He would take care of my relationships with others. According to Psalm 31:15, our times and seasons are in God's hands; He is the architect of time. This means that it was just a matter of time before He would intervene in my life and get all that He wanted and deserved from me. I realize now that God was long-suffering with me because He had ordered my steps and knew the way that I would take. Sure enough, in His own time, He used my life, with all its ups and downs, in addition to other people, with all their ways, to develop a hunger in me that could be filled only by Him.

An Unfulfilling Ministry

However, there were more battles to face before that time. Even though I had broken free of my church tradition where women weren't allowed to minister, there were still other insecurities to deal with. Although my ministry gifts had made room for me, I couldn't enjoy the room or completely walk out the gifts because I was not content.

God had gifted me to preach, teach, sing, and more. He then provided countless opportunities for me to use the gifts He had given. Invitations came. Engagements were accepted. God would show up and bless His people, but I would often end up feeling weary and disappointed. Sometimes I'd feel blessed. However, many times, I would feel used and abused, empty and unfulfilled, because I was laboring "for" and not "with" God. Some days I would catch myself leading in prayer without really praying, leading in praise without really praising, and preaching on autopilot to others, not really hearing the Word myself. I was running for Jesus—but I was running on empty.

Have you ever found yourself serving the Lord without gladness? Well, that is exactly where I was. I was giving my best in service, but like Martha, I was missing the *"good part"* that Mary got at Jesus' feet. (If you want to know more about the *"good part,"* read Luke 10:38–42.)

I had faith in God, but no faith in me. I began to focus on the things I had not mastered, instead of counting and being thankful for the things God had enabled me to accomplish. I listened to the enemy's voice instead of the voice of God inside of me and in His Word. As a result, I sank deeper and deeper into self-abasement and a negative self-image. I began to tell myself things like this: "Look at you! You are falling apart. You are getting slower and fatter, and now you even need glasses just to read." "Look at you. You can't swim after all these years." "Look at you! You've taken piano lessons and still can't play as well as you want to."

I should have stopped this negative talk, but I just kept hounding myself with defeating words like: "You'll never be rich." "You'll die an old maid." "People don't take you seriously as a preacher." "You're the laughingstock of your peers." I continuously spoke negative thoughts to myself until I was convinced that I would never excel in ministry. I told myself that I was inadequate and would never reach my dreams, so there was no real reason for me to try. At that point, the poisonous fear of failure had made its way to my heart and had started choking the life out of my dreams and throwing dirt on my faith in order to bury it.

I felt there were books in me that I wanted to write, but I was afraid that no one would want to read them. I desperately wanted to record some of the songs the Lord had given me, but I was afraid that no one would help me find a studio to record them. There were so many other dreams that I put on the back burner of my mind because of the fear of failure, dreams too numerous to discuss here. The fear of failure had such a stronghold on my life that I walked around in circles, only doing minor things that I knew I could master, like household chores, in order to *avoid making an effort* to do the things God was waiting to help me to do.

> The poisonous fear of failure had made its way to my heart and had started choking the life out of my dreams.

Delivered from Fear

Although I did have many wonderful leaders and loving role models to encourage me, something vital to my spiritual maturity and productivity was missing. It was at this point that the Lord brought a radically liberated, extremely anointed preacher into my life to gather me into the circle of his life and ministry. As a surrogate father, Bishop Jakes took me under his wings, with God's leading, and provided opportunities for me to minister and receive healing for myself. Through his ministry, I heard such messages as "We Are All Here," "A Satisfied Woman," "Ish," "Leftovers," and many, many more.

Each of these messages had its own medicine for the malady of my fear. For example, "We Are All Here" revealed the truth that all of us have been in bondage to something, even as the prisoners in the Philippian jail were in bondage. (See Acts 16:25–31.) Through this message, I realized that although everyone is not held captive by the same thing, it was important that I identify my own captor in order to be set free. So, I said out loud in prayer, "Lord, my captor is fear, but I want to be free!" Suddenly, I received the comforting knowledge that God's love and power were able to deliver *anyone*—including me—from anything that had him or her bound. It was equally as liberating to discover that being free meant I no longer had to run away from the fears I'd had in the past. On the contrary, now I could tell the story of my freedom and say, "That was me then, but look at me now!"

The impact that the message entitled "A Satisfied Woman" had on me is still very vivid. I especially remember being freed from all the words of friends, loved ones, and enemies alike who had constantly chided me for not being married. It seemed as if they thought I was a failure in life because I was still single. For a long time, I had pretended that what they said did not matter, but it did. It hurt me because I wanted to be accepted and acceptable. I smiled on the outside, but sank deeper and deeper into depression. Then, right in the middle of this message, I realized that I was what I was by the grace of God, and that, deep down, underneath the pain of all their words, I was really quite happy being single. The message reminded me that, as I delighted myself in the Lord and trusted in Him, He would give my heart the desires He wanted it to have, and would bring them to pass as I committed my way to Him (Psalm 37:4–5). This reaffirmed for me that I didn't have to prove anything to anyone. I didn't have to pine for Prince Charming in the natural, because I already had a Man, and His name is Jesus! It was such a liberating word that, from that day to this, I have been a satisfied woman!

The message entitled "Ish" took me to the next level of contentment, as it assured me of God's loving care as my Provider, Protector, and Friend. Through this message, God used the account of the marriage of Hosea to Gomer (who was a prostitute) to show me how far He would go to keep me as His own. I was sitting on the stage of the church at the time, and when Bishop Jakes came over, stood me up, and pulled me across the stage as an illustration of how God will come after you and pull you out of your misery into His all-sufficient love, I cried like a baby. That day, through that message, I truly became Jesus' bride, in my heart. *"For your Maker is your husband"* (Isaiah 54:5).

The message entitled "Leftovers" put the icing on my cake of freedom by showing me how God could use all of what He had done for me to bring glory to Him. He let me see how my previous struggles and even my mistakes could be turned from tragedies into testimonies. The text for this message was from 2 Kings 4, the wonderful story about the widow. It taught me that God wanted me to see that, after all I'd been through, He was not going to use what I had *lost,* but rather what I *still had,* in order to bless me, my family, and many others. The message made me take inventory of what I still had inside of me. When I did, I found that the oil of anointing is often squeezed out of struggles as a testimony to God's glory. I also learned that unless you are willing to pour out of your heart into others what the Lord has done for you, the blessing of who you have become will not be able to enrich the lives that God intends to send your way. It

> The oil of anointing is often squeezed out of our struggles.

was so inspiring to learn that God can and will take the leftovers of our lives, which start out as a mess, and turn them into a message that will bring life to others and glory to His name!

Each of these messages chipped away at my shackles until the phrase *"Woman, thou art loosed"* (Luke 13:12 KJV) became a reality in my life. At a certain point, I became free! Free from intimidation and fear, free from the futility of living to please others, free to be the real me.

Beloved, if fear has infected you with its poisonous bite, remember these drops of truth serum that helped me to walk out of its grip:

1. Fear is a spirit; it is like a snake that poisons and torments, and it does not come from God. (See 2 Timothy 1:7.)

2. Your fear not only hurts you, but it can also hurt the people around you. (See 1 Samuel 15:19–24.) Fear can spread to an entire nation. Stop it before it gets started. (See Psalm 37:1–3.)

3. The Word of God is your best source of truth serum. In it, God gives over 365 ways to defeat the spirit of fear. (See, for example, John 8:31–32.)

4. A heart that is guarded will not be invaded. (See Philippians 4:6–7.)

5. If your heart becomes infected, the perfect love of the Holy Spirit will cast out all fear. Receive His love! (See 1 John 4:18.)

Besides fear, there are many areas of bondage I could have been locked in, or locked up for, if it hadn't been for the grace of God. He protected me and freed me for a purpose, the same purpose He longs for you to enter into. Let's continue along the pathway, for on the next leg of the journey, God freed me to love…

...The Lover of My Soul

Chapter Two
The Lover of My Soul

No words could ever express how good it felt to be free, but now I had a new question. I was loosed, but loosed for what? I knew what I had been loosed from, but I didn't know what I had been loosed to do.

Now, the old saints had taught me that God never delivers us *from* something without delivering us *for* something, and that it's up to us to seek Him about what that something is. So I prayed and prayed until, by His grace, the Holy Spirit revealed the answer to me: *I had been loosed to love the Lover of my soul!*

The Lover of My Soul

I've loved the Lord Jesus Christ for as long as I can remember, beginning at the age of five. I remember singing "On a Hill Far Away" at my kindergarten graduation with tears streaming down my face, because as I sang about the old rugged cross, I knew He was real and I loved Him for loving me. I still cry every time I sing that old hymn. As a child, I had loved Him with all my heart, with as much as I then knew of love. That love, however, was now taking on a different meaning for me as His loosed woman. He began to show me the deeper dimensions of a relationship with Him that await us as we mature in Him. It's all about Him!

Jesus Wanted Me

The first truth He showed me, which melted my heart anew, was that He loved me so much that He wanted me. With all my faults, frailties, failures, and personality quirks, Jesus *wanted* me. I remember wondering as a teenager why all the guys I wanted didn't want me. (Of course, I wanted all the handsome ones, who were usually taken, and the only ones who seemed to want me were ugly to me. I know that beauty is in the eyes of the beholder, but after all, I was the one beholding! I'm glad I've since had a change of perspective.) The guys I liked always seemed to like someone else more, and they just thought of me as their "sister." Their sister? *Sister?* Can you believe that? Oh, well, looking back, I realize that when Jesus comforted my heart with the revelation that He truly wanted me, He also helped me to get over the rejection I had felt, brought healing to my emotions, renewed my self-esteem, and let me know it was their loss!

With all my faults, frailties, and failures, Jesus wanted me.

Jesus Waited for Me

Then Jesus taught me a second truth. Not only did He want me, but He had also *waited* for me. His long-suffering and protection in my early adulthood, and really for my entire life, had been extended to me because He knew the place and provision He had prepared for me. He patiently used every experience of my life, whether happy or sad, to bring me to an understanding of Jeremiah 29:11, which says, *"For I know the thoughts that I think toward you, says the LORD, thoughts of peace and not of evil, to give you a future and a hope."*

36

I think this verse summarizes God's feelings about us best, and the revelation of it humbled my heart, because so many of my childhood friends died prematurely. Some died in automobile accidents. Some died of drug overdoses. Some died of gunshot wounds. I remember one brilliant young man with tremendous potential. I had admired him in elementary school and wanted to be like him. Over the years, I lost touch with him, and then I found that he had tried to outwit some drug dealers during a drug transaction and was killed by them because of a dispute over just one dollar.

Other friends took their own lives. Some even died on the abortion table. Still others are alive but are like the walking dead. I remember another of my classmates whose friendship I enjoyed. We would talk about what we were going to do when we grew up and what we were going to become. Later, I found out that she had become strung out on heroin and was just walking the streets, never fulfilling the purpose that God had for her.

Many of these tragic stories are due to the fact that my friends got caught in an environment that perpetrated a cycle of destructive thinking and behavior. They were locked into circumstances that they couldn't or wouldn't leave, and many made wrong choices. Because I had become a Christian at an early age, and had a believing mother and grandmother who were praying for me, I believe that God's protection was on my life. I was delivered by the Lord from this bad environment when my mother married my stepfather and we moved away. If it weren't for the grace of God in removing my family from this environment, I might have gotten caught up in the same throes that destroyed the lives of my friends.

I grieve for the loss of these friends. I don't fully know why their lives ended up the way they did. We know that the Lord is *"not willing that any should perish but that all should come to repentance"* (2 Peter 3:9), and that the Lord's thoughts are good toward all of His creation. There are some things that we don't understand, which we have to leave to God. He gives us the right, the privilege, and the precious gift of choice—the attribute of will. When we choose Him, we experience a covering from that moment to the end of our earthly existence that actually shelters us from so many things—in spite of ourselves, in spite of mistakes that we might make, in spite of bad choices that we might make—because at that point, we are under His guardianship.

I want you to know that bad choices you've made in the past don't have to control your life now. I also made some bad choices in my life, but again, I believe my salvation as a young girl brought God's protection on me. Through this covering, as well as the prayers of my believing relatives, He guarded me, and through my wrong choices and my wandering from Him, through all of my life's experiences, He waited for me. He also waits for you now, whatever your past, however far you've run from Him. Know that He is waiting to receive you, save you, and bring you into His family.

Bad choices you've made in the past don't have to control your life now.

Sometimes He waits in the backgrounds of our lives for the moment when we are ready to receive Him. There's an analogy in the natural realm that might help to clarify this somewhat: A woman knows a guy who is very nice to her. He is a secret admirer but keeps it to himself. He is always hanging around, and when no one else will dance with her, she can always count on him to ask her. He is the friend who is there when she breaks up with some knucklehead who didn't really want her. He listens to her sad stories and helps her laugh. He picks her up when life deals her a blow. Then, one day, he gets up the nerve to express a more personal interest in her. She is in shock, but flattered, since he seems to have been waiting for the right time. She considers the possibility that it might work. After all, they are wonderful friends, so why not try a little romance?

In the natural, longtime friends sometimes become romantically involved, but other times, it doesn't work out. They try to kiss, but the "chemistry" that lights the fire of romance is missing. It's like kissing their brother or sister. Immediately, they know that they're not right for one another romantically. They find out that they're better off remaining wonderful friends. They want someone like each other, but with that certain attraction. So they end up standing in the lost-and-found department of love, waiting to be claimed by Mr. or Miss Wonderful, but life just doesn't seem to want to cooperate.

If that's been your experience, I feel for you, because that is exactly where I was, until I realized that Jesus was there all the time wanting me, waiting for me! And His love is the genuine thing. He is *the* One for you. *"Therefore the LORD will wait, that He may be gracious to you; and therefore He will be exalted, that He may have mercy on you"* (Isaiah 30:18). The consoling thing about Jesus' waiting is that He won't ever leave you. Hebrews 13:5 says, *"Let your conduct be without covetousness; be content with such things as you have. For He Himself has said, 'I will never leave you nor forsake you.'"*

This is a powerful commitment to me from the Lover of my soul, who has stayed with me through all of the "stuff" of my life. His express purpose was to bring me into the place of His anointing and grace. He remained faithful to me when I was unfaithful to Him. While I was trying life out, Jesus stayed by me and protected me. I experienced a lot of life before I slowed down enough to pay attention to His warning nudge. He sent His Holy

Spirit to hover over me and cover me in the midst of all the messy days and nights of my life. He showed me that He was my Redeemer and Friend. Then, finally, I allowed Him to become my Lord. Wow! What a moment that was! Jesus had waited to be gracious and merciful to me. After I had repented and surrendered all to Him, He blessed me. He did not force me, but He received me when I finally gave all of my heart to Him. Jesus had waited for me—*me!* Oh, how I love Him!

Jesus Continually Works in Me

Now, as if that weren't enough, the Holy Spirit gave me another "w" in the truths He was revealing to me. Besides *wanting* and *waiting*, I realized that Jesus had been *working* on me all the time. The same Jesus who went to Calvary to work for me, now works in me. He died to ensure that I would arrive at the place He'd reserved just for me.

As rotten as I was, in spite of all I had done, He was committed to working in me. He used His Word to convict, correct, and comfort me. He used His people to challenge, encourage, and mature me. He used life to delight, direct, and draw me closer to Him. The best part is, *"being confident of this very thing, that He who has begun a good work in* [me] *will complete it until the day of Jesus Christ"* (Philippians 1:6). In other words, when the Lord returns, I will be a completed masterpiece.

Jesus Watches Over Me

Then the Spirit of the Lord revealed an additional "w" to me: while God was working in me, He was also *watching* over me. The old saints used to sing, "All night, all day, angels watching over me, my Lord." When

I understood this truth in my life, I broke down and cried again, because I remembered the times when I should have been, could have been, would have been dead and gone, but for God's protection and interven- tion. His goodness and mercy have been following me all the days of my life. In a manner of speaking, you could say that the Lord has had His eye on me, like the sparrows. (See Matthew 10:29–31.) When I finally realized all these truths, I felt my heart fall in love all over again. I'd fallen in love, this time not just with Jesus the Christ, the Savior, the Son of God, but with Jesus the Lover of my soul!

I'd fallen in love not just with Jesus the Savior but with Jesus the Lover of my soul.

Loosed to Love Jesus

It was at this point that I understood all the mes- sages that I had heard or put into practice to be His way of *wooing* me. He let me know that He desired a level of intimacy with me that I needed, and that only He could provide.

What do I mean by intimacy? In dictionary terms, *intimacy* is familiarity, informal warmth, or privacy, as in a long-term friendship. However, the definition that flows out of my heart is this: Intimacy is knowing someone so well that I get a warm and fuzzy feeling when that person is around. I feel safe and secure enough to be my real self, because I wholly trust the person I am with to touch me in secret places without bruising the merchandise. Another definition for *intimacy* is "into me see," which indicates that a person sees into me, knows me, and still loves me. Well, this is how Jesus feels about me. He sees into me, and in spite of what He sees—moreover, because of what He knows about my past, present, and future—He still blesses me. He still keeps me. He is still committed to give me *"a future and a hope."* He still whispers to me, *"For I know the thoughts that I think toward you, says the* LORD, *thoughts of peace and not of evil, to give you a future and a hope"* (Jeremiah 29:11). He still loves me!

When I came to understand this truth, my soul then asked the question, "How do I express my love for Him and experience all the love and intimacy He has to give me? How can I share in the love and oneness that I so desperately need, the love and oneness that Jesus asked the Father to give to all of us who belong to Him?"

John 17:21 says, *"That they all may be one, as You, Father, are in Me, and I in You; that they also may be one in Us, that the world may believe that You sent Me."* Through this verse, I realized that Jesus was praying for me to experience intimacy with Him as His bride. As I prayed, the thought of Him being my Husband became very real to me. I accepted my role as His woman and set out to give the Man what He wanted! Although I've never been married, I believed that the Holy Spirit, through revelation and inspiration, could teach me daily how to enjoy an intimate relationship with Jesus. And that is what the Holy Spirit did.

Once my intimate relationship with Christ was established—once I was loosed to love Jesus—He enabled me to develop and deepen it through worship. This led to an unexpected result: as I continually lived a life of worship, He saturated me with His Spirit, and an overflow of divine life and purpose poured out from me to others. I am now living in the fullness and abundance of life that Christ came to give us. The same thing can happen to you. You also can be...

PART II
...Loosed to Love Jesus

Part II:
Loosed to Love Jesus

Embracing Him

"We love Him because He first loved us" (1 John 4:19). God has loosed us from bondage. He has loosed us to love Him and to receive all of the indescribable riches that He has for us. When we recognize how much God loves us, and all that He's done for us, we're so grateful that we desire to love Him back with all of our hearts.

That's where I was at the beginning of my pathway to intimacy. That's where I want to take you now, as I share with you how I learned to love the Lover of my soul, and how He has transformed and continues to transform my life through my intimate encounters with Him.

First of all, I had to decide that...

...I Really Do Want
to Satisfy Him

Chapter Three

I Really Do Want to Satisfy Him

Once I understood that I was loosed to love, I asked myself, "If Jesus were here (and He is), would I work to satisfy Him?" The answer was a resounding "Yes!" Now, if anyone were to ask me *why* I was willing to satisfy Him, I would simply tell them that His love and care for me have surpassed what anyone else has ever given me. No one else has put up with my ways and been so loving. No one else has dried tears I've shed over another love. He has spoiled me so, until I will gladly work to satisfy Him by doing whatever He asks.

My motivation for serving is His great love for me. As a result of His love, my heart is filled with so much gratitude that I have to find a way of expressing my love for Him. Otherwise, I might find myself channeling all the love I feel for Christ toward someone else, and that would be idolatry. Please don't misunderstand me. We should express our love to others in all the godly ways that are available to us. We just have to make sure that we make God our first love.

My motivation for serving is His great love for me.

49

Expressing My Love for God

All of us need to be able to express our love for others, although we don't all do it in the same way. Sometimes we show love by just being there for someone, by serving, or by giving gifts. We can even show our love by the care we put into a well-prepared meal. A beautifully presented culinary delight is always a pleasure to our palates and our hearts. We also show love by how much quality time we spend with someone. When we are romantically involved, we sometimes spend huge amounts of time thinking about our special someone. We rush to the telephone when our loved one calls, hurry home to him or her, buy flowers, or send cards, candy, or balloons—all to show that special someone how much he or she is loved. Again, we just have to make sure that we give God our love first. Deuteronomy 6:5 says, *"You shall love the LORD your God with all your heart,"* and Exodus 20:3 says, *"You shall have no other gods before Me."*

After I had established *why* I wanted to satisfy Him, I asked myself, *"When* should I show Him my love? When do I have time to love Him?" I must confess that, in the past, I allowed my life to become so demanding at times that I barely had time for myself. I found myself going to labor for Him, without having spent time with Him. Although others may have been blessed, this type of neglect created a void in my life that poignantly reminded me that I needed what He provided more than anything, and I needed it all the time. I made little time for rest, little time for exercise and health maintenance, little if any time for fun and frolic, and very little time for Him. I must have been crazy, right? Today I know that I want His love just as much as He wants mine. Consequently, I need to be ready at all times to give Him anything He wants.

I can testify that He has always been right there whenever I've called His name. Surely, it's not too much for me to be there whenever He calls mine. Wait a minute. I just heard Jesus whisper my name. His voice is gently brushing my inner soul, causing my spirit to come alive with passion for Him. Excuse me while I go and see what He wants. I'll be right back...

Okay, I'm back, and no, I am not going to tell you all He said. However, I will tell you that anytime you hear Him calling you while you're reading this book, please go ahead and spend time with Him, listening to what He has to say. It will be worth the interruption, and I'll be here when you get back!

My Knight in Shining Armor

I once had a fantasy when I was a little girl. My knight in shining armor would ride up in a white limousine (like a movie I saw recently) and sweep me away. He'd be tall and handsome. He would have broad shoulders and sensitive hands; he would be brilliant; and he would be very, very rich. He'd be my Boaz, as in the book of Ruth. And, like Ruth, I'd meet the man of my dreams while doing the will of my God.

Real life, however, has been different for me so far. I haven't met my husband, but I have met my Knight. He didn't come riding in a limousine, but He came walking down through forty-two generations of the people of God from the time of Abraham to His birth in Bethlehem. He didn't climb the stairs to my balcony to bring me down to him, but He did climb the hill called Calvary to reach me and bring me up to His Father. Jesus proved His love for me—and you—at the cross. There He released my heart from the pain of past loves that had hurt the woman in me. Thank God I am no longer hurt. In this relationship

51

with Jesus, I receive all that He gives, and He never rejects me. He is my Love, the Lover of my soul, my Heart, my Beloved! There is not an hour or a moment that I don't feel His love, and every day I try to make sure He can say the same for me. My love is sealed forever in the bond of unity that I have found with Him.

So if I really want to satisfy Jesus, and I do, then any time, starting right now, is the perfect time to show love to the Lover of my soul. But your soul may be asking, as mine did, how you can do this. "How can I satisfy someone who *is* satisfaction personified? How do I bring a smile to the face of the One who is already altogether lovely? How can I let Him know how much He means to me? How can I show Him how much I long to experience intimacy with Him?"

There is not an hour or a moment that I don't feel His love.

I Want You

This is the answer I found: Start by telling Him, "I want You." My heart is like the deer of Psalm 42:1: *"As the deer pants for the water brooks, so pants my soul for You, O God."* The word *"pants"* may also be translated *longs* or *lusts.* Now, *lusts* may seem to be a strong word, or may even seem to be out of place here. However, there is such a thing as pure lust (strong desire). Pure lust can be a good thing if it comes from a pure heart and is channeled in the right direction. For a long time, I thought of lust with only a negative connotation because my desires had been perverted. Yes, I admit it. I had abused this desire in the past by lusting after people that I could not have or longing for things I did not really need. After suffering many disappointments, I finally realized that intimacy with Jesus is what my soul was desiring all along. Now, every time I think of it, I make it a point to tell Him that He is my heart's desire. I let Him know that I long lustfully to show Him how much He is worth to me.

By the way, we show how much things or people are worth to us by the way we treat them. For example, we show that our cars or homes have worth to us by taking good care of them. Changing the oil in our cars and cleaning our kitchens are both ways of showing the value of God's gifts to us. We also reveal the worth of our loved ones to us by the way we care for them. Buying them clothes or doing whatever is necessary to provide for their needs shows their value to us. God doesn't mind, as long as we don't allow our love for them to supercede our love for Him!

I will discuss this idea in more detail later, but it is important to note here that the act of showing true "worth-ship" is defined by the word *worship.* People express worship in many ways, but for me, worship is what happens when I move from praise (speaking well about God to others) to doting on Him and speaking well of Him to Him. This communion is face-to-face, heart-to-heart, and ultimately, spirit-to-Spirit.

Sometimes I just sit and tell Him that He is awesome, that there is none like Him, that He is tremendous. And when I run out of English words to say, I let His Spirit inside me finish complimenting Him with the *"tongues of men and of angels"* (1 Corinthians 13:1). Romans 8:26 says, *"The Spirit Himself makes intercession for us with groanings which cannot be uttered."* The Holy Spirit helps me say what is in my heart, including all that my vocabulary cannot articulate. The Lord enjoys hearing the love flowing from my heart, and my heart gets great joy from telling Him of my love, because every word of it is true. Through worship, I find out over and over again that I really do love and long for Jesus, who is the Lover of my soul.

Setting the Mood

Now, I have learned through my natural experiences that the coals of intimacy can be ignited by the sound of soft music, which melts the heart. Intimacy also can be kindled by the warmth of a crackling fire, the caress of a gentle touch, or the flickering light of a solitary candle.

The spiritual counterparts to these things all help to set the mood for an intimate encounter with the Lord. I want Jesus' undivided attention, and I want Him to have mine. I take the time to prepare for our intimate exchange by making sure the atmosphere is filled with love and expectation. My heart's desire is to usher in the presence of my Lord. In anticipation of His arrival, I light the fireplace of my heart with mood music that compliments Him. Not just any music will do. There is a special kind of music that speaks lovingly of His name, His nature, His ways, and His acts. Some people call this praise and worship music, but I lovingly call it my mood music. I turn it on and sing along; before I know it, He makes His tender presence known as He enters the room.

The Lord enjoys hearing the love flowing from my heart, and I get great joy from telling Him of my love.

I have found that an encounter with Jesus can occur when I am in church, or it can happen when I am in my living room, kitchen, basement, or bathroom; it can happen in the car, on a train, on a bus, on a plane, or even while I'm walking or sitting. Wherever the "mood" is right, and the atmosphere of praise and worship has been set, the Lord Jesus Christ will show up; and whenever He shows up, our intimate exchange begins. I have, on many occasions, even had to pull my car to the side of the road when He has shown up! The presence of Jesus fills the air and takes my breath away as I embrace Him. There are times when my eyes well up with tears because of the remembrance of His great love.

Most of the time, however, I feel closest to Him when I sing to Him upon my bed. I think the psalmist must have felt the same way. Psalm 149:5 tells us, *"Let the saints be joyful in glory; let them sing aloud on their beds,"* and Psalm 63:5–7 says, *"My mouth shall praise You with joyful lips. When I remember You on my bed, I meditate on You in the night watches. Because You have been my help, therefore in the shadow of Your wings I will rejoice."* Verse seven in the New International Version reads, *"Because you are my help, I sing in the shadow of your wings."*

Maybe I feel closest to Him then because at night, or when I'm resting, I quiet my heart and mind from the busyness and pressures of the day, and I concentrate on Him fully. I have time to think of all He has done to help me, and as I do, I am filled with gratitude and praise for Him! Night is also a time when many believers, myself included, cry out to God about our troubles:

> *I cry out with my whole heart; hear me, O LORD! I will keep Your statutes. I cry out to You; save me, and I will keep Your testimonies. I rise before the dawning of the morning, and cry for help; I hope in Your word. My eyes are awake through the night watches, that I may meditate on Your word.*
> (Psalm 119:145–148)

And so, I intimately commune with the Lord upon my bed and enjoy the comfort, strength, and love He gives me during our times of fellowship.

Making a Joyful Noise

Perhaps you are a person who sings in the shower. Even if you feel that you can't carry a tune, know that, for some reason, God just loves to hear us make a joyful noise. He can hear us making melody in our hearts. When our hearts become full of our love melody, it spills out of our lips and makes its way to Him. If you have never sung to the Lord as a way of showing your love for Him, try it—you'll like it, and so will He!

Don't Break the Mood

Please be aware that, although worship seems like an innocent, harmless thing to do, the enemy hates it when I sing to Jesus, because of the great joy and strength that I receive. So the enemy tries to crowd my head with thoughts that will break the mood (he'll try to do the same to you). He sends messages, as thoughts to my mind, reminding me of my mistakes and shortcomings, faults and failures, or even forgotten tasks. Don't let him do this to you. Resist! (See James 4:7.)

Fluffing the Pillows of Your Mind

If I give in and listen to the enemy, it will destroy the mood; but I'm determined not to let him win, so I just take charge and "fluff the pillows of my mind."

Psalm 139:14 tells me that *"I am fearfully and wonderfully made."* Translated into modern terms, this means that I am tremendous and terrific—body, spirit, and soul. My body is such a work of art, and yet it is so intricately constructed that it can, by God's design, even heal itself. My spirit, the inner me, allows me to commune with the true and living God, sometimes without even saying a word. But the third part of me, my soul, is just as miraculous as my body and spirit. My soul contains my emotions, my will, and my reasoning abilities. My soul contains my mind!

Now, the mind is a very powerful instrument in any arena. But when true intimacy is desired, I've discovered that you can "fluff the pillows of your mind" and set your mind's affections. You can tune in your thoughts so completely upon the object of your love that nothing can stop or even hinder the flow of love that is being shared between you. I'm a witness that you can block out everything else completely, turn your mind on "receive" mode, and get all that the Lord Jesus has to give. Just like concentration opens one up to really receive in the natural course of lovemaking, meditating upon Jesus opens the heart to receive true spiritual intimacy.

You can tune your thoughts so completely upon Jesus that nothing can hinder the flow.

Then, simply by fluffing the pillows of your mind again, you can go into "give" mode and lavish Him with all that is in your heart to give. Fluffing the pillows of our minds by setting our affections on Him can be a strong defense against the arrows of the enemy that come to steal precious moments of intimacy from us. Colossians 3:2 says, *"Set your mind on things above, not on things on the earth."* When I follow the instruction of this verse, I become overwhelmed by His heavenly love. What wonderful moments I experience! In the ecstasy of these moments, I may laugh out loud. I may cry. I may clap my hands with the joy of gladness and contentment.

To capture these moments, I have learned that it is very important to regularly put on fresh pillowcases (refresh your mind with His Word) and fluff the pillows again (meditate), because fluffing works every time. A good place to start refreshing your mind and meditating is Philippians 4:8, which says,

Whatever things are true, whatever things are noble, whatever things are just, whatever things are pure, whatever things are lovely, whatever things are of good report, if there is any virtue and if there is anything praiseworthy; meditate on these things.

If you want to get your head in the right place, *"meditate on these things,"* because these things describe the Lover of our souls to a tee.

Saturated in His Presence

May I let you in on a secret? When I take the time to really fluff the pillows of my mind and meditate, or think on Him, it's not unusual for me to shed tears in worship. When I recount the many times He has preserved me, I am blown away with the emotion of a satisfying love, and the tears come. *"If it had not been the LORD who was on [my] side..."* (Psalm 124:1).

I can look back and see God's protection throughout my life. I remember the time when I was a child, and I dived into a pool at the three-foot-deep end, hit my head on the bottom of the pool, and jumped straight up out of the water unharmed. Then there was the time I was near a lawn mower that kicked up a rock at high speed. The rock hit me squarely on my right temple, doing no real damage except to my ego. The outcome surely could have been far worse! About two years ago, I was in an accident in which two eighteen-wheeler trucks collided, came across the highway, and totaled my six-week-old Mark VIII Lincoln, with me sitting in the driver's seat. The only thing that was preserved was the seat in which I was sitting. I had been listening to Vicki Winans' song, "He's More than Enough" when all of this transpired. God's angels shielded me from any injury whatsoever.

These are but a few of the many visible dangers, not to mention unseen dangers, through which He has kept me. So when these and many other instances of His miraculous love come to my mind, my heart fills up with thanksgiving and my eyes start leaking praise. In other words, I become wet with tears of joy! This causes me to have an openness to God through which He ministers to me.

Now, if we are honest, we have to admit that wetness does make it easier for an intimate exchange between a husband and wife. So it is in the Spirit. Through my tears of joy, I experience the kind of inner saturation that makes me feel that I am one with Christ. When my heart is throbbing in response to His mighty touch, I am bone of His bone and flesh of His flesh; I'm in Him and He's in me. I am one with Him, and in that moment, we share real intimacy.

Yet there are times when my tears are not tears of joy. I can truly say that I have cried many sorrowful tears at night just before receiving a breakthrough. I've cried myself to sleep over a broken heart. I've cried over the loss of a loved one. I've cried when sharing the burden of someone else. However, whether I was crying tears of joy or tears of sadness, tears of praise or tears of pain, all my tears have brought me closer to Christ.

Most assuredly, I have never been ashamed to cry, and I can truly say that all the tears of my life have, in some way, watered my heart and prepared me for a breakthrough to another level of intimacy with Christ. Beloved, Psalm 30:5 is so true when it says, *"For His anger is but for a moment, His favor is for life; weeping may endure for a night, but joy comes in the morning."* I want to emphasize that, in the good times and the bad, weeping that endures for the night prepares you for ecstasy, intimacy, and joy in the morning. In appropriating this truth, it is important to remember that even though morning doesn't always come as quickly as we would like, we can still rejoice in hope (Romans 12:12) because morning *will* come, and when it comes, joy will come with it.

Count It All Joy

Experiencing these different types of tears and how God uses them in my life is how I have learned that all things are working together for my good. Romans 8:28 says, *"And we know that all things work together for good to those who love God, to those who are the called according to His purpose."* Down through the years, and through all the tears, I've learned to trust the purpose of God and depend on Jesus more and more. I understand what James meant when he said in James 1:2, *"My brethren, count it all joy when you fall into various trials."* This is just another way of saying that all of us will have different tests, but we should reckon that joy will come in spite of them. "Counting it all joy" will allow us to feel comfort in calamity, safety in storms, and trust in the times of our tearful tests. Thank God that I have learned this important truth. Now, no matter which tears may come, I've matured enough in Christ to know that...

> Counting it all joy will allow us to feel comfort in calamity, safety in storms, and trust in times of tearful tests.

...He Can Be Trusted

Chapter Four

He Can Be Trusted

Sometimes, when you've been hurt by people, whether in life or in love, it's difficult to let go and love again. It's hard to trust that you won't be hurt yet another time. This is especially true of women—and, yes, my thinking is affected by my femininity. Perhaps I am more cautious because I am a woman, and women usually hold on to pain longer than men. Nevertheless, the truth is that all of us have been hurt by someone at some time.

Unfortunately, it is the nature of humankind that we hurt one other. It's not even always intentional, but human trust is such a fragile chord that it usually only takes being once burned to be twice shy. Being burned in life or love produces a kind of hesitancy that often causes us to hold back emotionally. Let me warn you, however, that if you are trying to achieve intimacy with Jesus, this twice shy, holding back, slow-to-trust attitude can keep you from really getting all the joy, peace, and satisfaction that should accompany His presence in your life.

Often, people lose our trust because they don't have a good track record with us. They've failed us in some way, and as a result, we have cut off their access to intimacy with us. We can never lay this charge against God, however, because His track record is perfect. In fact, if the truth be told, He is the only One whose track record is perfect. That's because He is perfect. People have failed us over and over again. We have failed others and ourselves over and over again. And what about our track record with God? Well, frankly, we ought to throw up both of our hands and constantly thank God for not counting our failures and not holding our track record against us. What amazing grace has been given to us!

So many times, I've gone back to Him asking His forgiveness for the same sin. I have been sincerely sorry for my sin, and meant never to do it again. Somehow, however, I would find myself right back where I had been, doing again what I had done—you know, living out Romans 7:21, which, to paraphrase, says, "When I want to do good, evil is always present." If God had dealt with me according to my sin, I don't know where I would be now. Can you testify to that in your own life? But He never once gave up on me. He never stopped working on me. He never stopped leading me with love, until His love and goodness finally led me to true repentance, which caused me to forsake that particular sin. This process is repeated in my life over and over for each sin that He reveals to me.

As many times as I know I've disappointed Him, I can honestly say that He's been there for me my whole life. He has always been busy opening doors, making ways, pouring out blessings, and proving over and over again that He really can be trusted to love and perfect me.

Today, I'm a witness along with the apostle Paul, who said in 2 Timothy 1:12, *"For this reason I also suffer these things; nevertheless I am not ashamed, for I know whom I have believed and am persuaded that He is able to keep what I have committed to Him until that Day."* I feel like the old saints who used to sing the hymn "Trust and Obey."

Beloved, I believe that trust is a secret ingredient in intimacy. Trust allows me to open myself fully to Him, and give Him access to rule over the innermost parts of my being. In other words, because I trust Him not to hurt me, I can tell Him, "Into me see' (intimacy). Take all of me. Do what You will. Have Your way, Jesus."

> Trust is a secret ingredient in intimacy with Christ.

Penetrate Me

This is my heart's earnest desire, so I prepare myself to let go completely and let the Lover of my soul penetrate me.

I never will forget the first time a young man penetrated me naturally and cost me my virginity. At the point of penetration, my hymen broke, and blood was shed that should have been reserved for covenant consummation on my wedding night. I wish I had known then what I know now.

Even though I blew it big time, the God of all grace, indeed the Lover of my body, soul, and spirit, forgave me of my sin because of the sacrifice of His Son, Jesus, my Kinsman Redeemer. Then Jesus restored my soul by showing me that the real covenant consummation was wrought through the shedding of His own blood on Calvary. He revealed to me that, by receiving Him and inviting Him to fill me with Himself, He would penetrate my spirit with His Spirit, cover me with His blood, and declare me to be His chaste virgin. Hallelujah!

Well, beloved, let me take you back to the day that I took Him up on His offer. It was about midnight on a hot Sunday in August. I had tried to be reserved, and had refused to praise the Lord at the bidding of some wise old saints. I just knew it didn't take all that praising in order to reach Him. I let pride and tradition keep me closed off from Him for hours. Then, finally, one old mother said to me, "If you really want Him, call His name and ask Him to fill you!" At that point, I began to feel a longing that could be satisfied only by having His fullness inside all of me. It was then that I opened my mouth wide and cried, "Fill me, Lord. Penetrate me by Your Spirit and fill me up with Your presence."

I became lost in my desire and began to praise Him and call His name. I said, "Je— Je— Je— Jesus, Jesus, Jesus," until I began to feel His Spirit breaking through the pride of life in me—breaking through my inhibitions and my traditional past. All of a sudden, the hymen of my pride broke within me, and the grace of His blood overwhelmed me. The floodgates of my soul opened, and up out of my own heart came rivers of living water. The words "Hallelujah!" "Glory!" and "Thank You, Jesus!" gave way to utterances that had no English translation at that moment.

I didn't realize it then, but I had just stepped into a new realm of praise. It was my own experience of Isaiah 28:11, which says, *"For with stammering lips and another tongue He will speak to this people."* It was indeed a rest and refreshing to my soul. My stammering lips released what seemed to me like baby talk—gibberish that made no sense in the natural.

However, those utterances in His presence bathed my soul and released my spirit to a spiritual climax that has no equal in the natural. I've experienced waves of spiritual climaxes from that day to this. As a matter of fact, I feel Him penetrating and saturating me right now.

Take Me Where I've Never Gone Before

It may be unorthodox to write about spiritual experiences in this way, but the pathway to intimacy is such that the Lover of my soul has access to me all along the way. Anytime He wants to, He can have me for His pleasure and take me where I've never gone before.

Nobody can satisfy me like Jesus! Just when I think I have experienced all the joy I can handle, He takes me to another level of joy. Just when I think I have found the peace that passes all understanding, He gives me another dimension of peace that leaves me marveling over His ways. And just when I think I'm so blessed that I couldn't ask for anything more, He blows my mind with blessings, favors, and benefits that take me to higher heights and deeper depths in Him!

Because of Christ, I enjoy life, and that more abundantly (John 10:10). My needs are met. My heart's desires are granted. I feel no lack! Each day is an adventurous journey with so many wonderful places to visit between sunrise and sunset. It's not unusual for me to take a praise break at any time, just to tell Him how much He means to me.

Through intimacy with Christ, I have experienced a greater love for Him, for myself, and for others. This is part of what I mean when I say that He takes me where I've never been before. I find that I am much more patient with myself. In fact, I have become one of my biggest fans. I finally love myself enough to take care of myself and even sometimes to pamper myself. As for others, now I am willing to go farther to show my love for them. I enjoy letting the love of God be seen and felt through me. I no longer give love in order to get love; I give love because He keeps giving me love to give.

> I give love because He keeps giving me love to give.

He loved me first; then He showed me how to love Him; and now He's teaching me how to love myself. The result is that I've been given a tremendous capacity for loving others—people I don't even know, people I haven't met, people I've never seen. Bishop Jakes told me when he first hired me to facilitate at his conferences, "I hired you because you love God, you love God's Word, and you love people. If you have these three elements going for you, you're going to be successful in the kingdom." He was right!

God has given me a love that allows me to be open, and not intimidated, to love others. I never used to want to tell people that I loved them because I was afraid that they would reject me. But when I feel God's love, it's something that I cannot really deny. I can't explain it, and I can't explain it away. So, rather than try to hide from it, or pretend that it's not there, I just let it flow. And what I've found is that, because I have learned to love Jesus more, I can more easily let His love go out to people without worrying about whether it's coming back or how it's being received. I just give it because I have it to give.

I think that intimacy with Jesus moves us to another level of the fruit of the Spirit. Of course, everything starts with love. Love is the sap that circulates through all of the attributes and fruit of the Spirit. It is the motivating factor that goes through all of them.

Through the love that God has given me, He has made me much more patient and much more merciful. His love has shown me how much mercy He's extended to me—how patient, how long-suffering, how tender He's been with me. This has made me much more tolerant of others and much less judgmental.

I also know that I'm more tender in my dealings with others, and more consistent in saying "I love you" and showing "I love you" to others by doing little things so that people know that I really, really care. I find that I can contribute to people's well-being by touching and hugging them, because the sense of touch is important for both mental and physical health.

In addition, I find that I have a real sensitivity to older people, because they are in the twilight of their years and many of them are not experiencing what they thought they were going to have in life. They haven't fulfilled what they wanted to do, and in some cases, they are left alone to fend for themselves—they are almost relegated to second-class citizenry. They have given so much love, they've sacrificed for so many years, but now many of them have children or grandchildren who never come to see them. What a sad commentary. If those who neglect their elders live long enough, they may reap what they have sown, having no one to love or care for them when they grow old. (See Galatians 6:7.) Ephesians 6:2–3 says, *"Honor your father and mother,' which is the first commandment with promise: 'that it may be well with you and you may live long on the earth,'"* and Leviticus 19:32 says, *"You shall rise before the gray headed and honor the presence of an old man, and fear your God: I am the* LORD.*"* We should give love to our parents and grand-parents out of a desire to honor our elders and our God.

I have also stretched my borders and opened myself to *receive* more love than ever before. In doing so, I have discovered a road of endless supply because of Him. He not only provides what I need, He *is* what I need.

His Love Is So Real

Because of Christ, I'm willing to go the last mile of the way for His glory. I'm not ashamed to preach His Gospel or lift up His name or bear my cross for Him. Wherever I go, I receive great joy from serving Him; and I'll go anywhere for Him, because His love is so real.

What I have been describing about intimacy with Christ is not unusual for those who are His bride. I'm not crazy! When I'm lost in His presence and loving Him with all my heart, and as He loves me with the fullness of who He is, nothing in the whole world is more real or more powerful. I'm in Him, He's in me, and oneness is what I feel. It is very hard to know where He ends and I start, or where I end and He begins. Just as a happily married husband and wife become one flesh through physical intimacy (Genesis 2:23–24), Jesus and I, through spiritual intimacy, become one in His Spirit. In Him, I become whole, and what I feel is not imagined. It's real!

The oneness that I have with Christ gives me a settled security that allows me to rest from laboring according to my flesh, and to trust His love and care for me. Just as I entered His rest for my salvation, I also receive a rest from daily struggles through intimacy with Him. Sometimes, when I just sit still, His presence is so powerfully manifested that I'll find myself talking out loud to Him, knowing that He hears me. Then I'll smile or laugh out loud, knowing that if someone else were to see or hear me, they would think that I was crazy.

At other times, His presence is so rich that natural communication, such as singing, waving, shouting, or dancing is completely inadequate to express how I feel about Him, because He and I have gone beyond the natural to the supernatural. I believe that this is what John meant when he said, *"God is Spirit, and those who worship Him* [who love Him and show forth His worth] *must worship in spirit and truth"* (John 4:24).

I can't allow myself to be inhibited in any way when I'm loving (worshiping) the Lover of my soul. He's looking for real love from a real person. There is no time or place for pretense or hypocrisy. What He sees, inside and out, is what He gets. I may not be able to share all of who I am with anyone else (people can't always handle who we really are), but I can be the "real me" with Jesus. Thank God!

Afterglow

Now, after all is said and done, when love is truly given from a sincere heart, the act of worshiping, loving, and sharing intimacy with Christ leaves its own afterglow.

In the natural, there is usually something about a person's countenance that indicates they have been intimate with someone. It is not unusual to see a kind of glow on the face, a little sparkle in the eye, a smug snicker here and there, a smile that will not go away. These are all telltale signs of an intimate exchange. In the natural world, this is known as the "afterglow" of lovemaking.

As it is in the natural, so it is in the spiritual. As we share intimacy with Jesus, who is the true Lover of our souls, we are left with His afterglow. Now, His afterglow is hard to hide, too, because it is the reflection of an awesome experience with an extraordinary God that has left an indelible imprint upon our lives. Once we sincerely and completely have given ourselves over to His love, we will never be or look the same again. I believe that one of the most beautiful sights in the whole world is the face of a brand-new convert as he or she receives Christ. And I have found that a lifestyle of worship will keep generating the same afterglow day after day after day, for an entire lifetime.

Once we have given ourselves over to His love, we will never be the same again.

The afterglow that comes from my intimate exchange with the Lover of my soul leaves me with the desire to keep touching Him. I can't get enough of touching Him, because He keeps touching me back. I keep touching Him with a song or another form of praise, and He keeps giving me satisfaction guaranteed. In the afterglow, many times I want to linger longer than my earthly schedule allows. I have often had to adjust my schedule altogether, just for Him. But guess what? I don't mind at all, because righteousness, peace, joy, and contentment accompany His afterglow.

Whether I experience midnight deliverance or early morning dew, the afterglow of His love is something that changes me forever. According to 2 Corinthians 3:18, *"We all, with unveiled face, beholding as in a mirror the glory of the Lord, are being transformed into the same image from glory to glory, just as by the Spirit of the Lord."* The old saints used to say it this way: "I know I've been changed!"

With every intimate exchange I share with Jesus, I feel myself growing and becoming a better me. On the pathway to intimacy, I gain a deeper relationship with Him all the time, because my love for Him becomes stronger and more precious. One reason for this increased love is that, at the same time I've been loosed to love, I've also been...

PART III
...Loosed for True Worship

Part III:

Loosed for True Worship

Pathway to Intimacy

In Part II, "Loosed to Love Jesus," I talked about how God taught me to love Him in a deep and intimate way. I want you to know that you also can experience this loving relationship with the Lover of your soul as you walk the pathway that leads to intimacy, the pathway of true and genuine worship. What's more, if you take this pathway, you'll enter into a new understanding of the purposes that He has for your life. In Part IV, we will talk about how to find and fulfill these purposes of God.

When you're loosed to love Jesus, you're loosed to worship Him in a way that enhances and deepens your love relationship with Him. To travel the pathway of intimacy, we need to understand the *pattern* of worship, the *posture* of worship, and the *perfection* of worship. Through the pattern, which is based on the spiritual realities of the tabernacle of Moses, we will learn how God wants us to worship Him. Through the posture, we will see how worship is to become our lifestyle. Then, as worship becomes our way of life, we will understand how it is to be perfected. That is to say, as we mature in worship, we will be able to love and live in unity with others, as well as God, and become extremely effective as kingdom workers because of our relationship with Him.

The temple of Solomon, with its emphasis on unity, then becomes our model as we move into the perfection of worship.

The pattern, the posture, and the perfection of worship take us from the initial experience of worship, through the consistent practice of worship in our daily lives that will bring us into a mature revelation of what worship truly means. As we develop in our understanding and practice of worship, it is going to be walked out in our lives, and we will be filled with the glory of God, as the temple of Solomon was on the day of dedication. (See 2 Chronicles 7:1–2.) The temple was immaculate, exquisite, and excellent—there was nothing but the best everywhere. That's really what I believe the Lord is leading us to—a life of excellence, a life of brilliance, a life of total maturity that expresses His love and allows the glory of God to be seen in us as we walk out the life of Christ. With this in mind, let us prepare to enter into the tabernacle of Moses and discover the meaning of...

...The Outer Court and the Holy Place

Chapter Five

The Outer Court and the Holy Place

Beloved, let us remember that we have been loosed *from* something so that we can be loosed *for* something. The reason we have been loosed is found in Matthew 22:37–39:

> *"You shall love the LORD your God with all your heart, with all your soul, and with all your mind." This is the first and great commandment. And the second is like it: "You shall love your neighbor as yourself."*

We have been loosed for love: genuine love for God and for our neighbors.

True love, whether for God, ourselves, or our neighbors, starts with devotion to God, and we have both the right and the responsibility to praise and worship Him as an expression of our love. We seek His face because we love Him. Once we have been loosed from bondage and the issues of our lives have been dealt with (or are being dealt with), then our emotions can come into alignment so that we can love Him with our whole beings. In the past, we were distracted by the bondages we were in. Now that we are loosed, our souls can cling to the Lord with all our intellect, strength, and God-given abilities.

The Truth of Worship

I want to show you a pattern for worship that will help you to love God with your whole being as you travel the pathway of intimacy with Him. You can experience the same intimacy with God that He has enabled me to have if you will follow the pathway that leads to intimacy, which is true worship.

True worship leads to intimacy.

Before we discuss this pattern for worship, however, let's look at a Scripture text that is foundational to all we will be learning about true worship:

> *The hour is coming, and now is, when the true worshipers will worship the Father in spirit and truth; for the Father is seeking such to worship Him. God is Spirit, and those who worship Him must worship in spirit and truth.* (John 4:23–24)

"The hour is coming, and now is." This is the hour when the Father is seeking true worshipers—those who will worship Him *"in spirit and truth."*

Let's consider what it means to be a true worshiper. The word *worship* originally came from the combination of two Old English words, *weorth,* meaning "worthy" or "worth," and *scipe,* meaning "ship." Taking these original meanings, the word means to show the "worth-ship" of a person or thing. To express or celebrate or magnify the worth of a person or thing is what worship, in its truest definition, is all about.

God wants us to understand that all of us as created beings were made to worship Him. We have the equipment that is necessary for worship: hearts, minds, souls, bodies, and spirits. Yet a large number of people worship many things other than God and miss the One who is to be the true object of our worship. Revelation 4:11 says, *"You are worthy, O Lord."* Notice that the verse says, *"**You** are worthy."* There is nobody beside Him, nobody above Him, nobody behind Him. *"You are worthy, O Lord."*

We Were Made for God's Pleasure

The full verse reads, *"You are worthy, O Lord, to receive glory and honor and power; for You created all things, and by Your will ["pleasure," KJV] they exist and were created."* That is a powerful, powerful truth. God has created all things for His pleasure. I was made to make God happy; I was made to make Him smile; I was made to make Him grin. When you praise Him, He just lights up. He sings; He glories over you. *"The LORD thy God in the midst of thee is mighty; he will save, he will rejoice over thee with joy; he will rest in his love, he will joy over thee with singing"* (Zephaniah 3:17 KJV).

So we were made to glorify Him, to make Him happy, to bring Him pleasure. And one of the ways we bring Him pleasure is to tell Him how worthy He is, how awesome He is, how there isn't anybody like Him. You know what happens when somebody compliments you—you get a big head, and you get a smile on your face, even if what the person said about you isn't true. But God's worthiness is true. Everything good we can say about Him is true.

He is worthy to receive *"blessing and honor and glory and power"* (Revelation 5:13). Let us bless the Lord. Let us give Him glory. Let us ascribe honor to Him. Even if we didn't have tongues, we could still give Him glory, because every part of us was made to bring Him glory.

You can give Him glory with your hands. When you give Him glory with your hands, you will be able to feel the power that comes from honoring Him, even though you don't use words. Something will happen inside you, and you won't even have to be able to articulate it.

The devil gets upset when we praise the Lord because he was the archangel of worship; he was in charge of worship; he was supposed to be the chief worship leader. Then he got a big head, rebelled against God, and took a third of the angels with him. (See Isaiah 14:13–15; Revelation 12:3–4.) But he was created to make music. Before his rebellion, every time he moved, the music that his pipes and harp made was perfect. Whenever he moved, he gave worship to God.

We as believers should worship the Eternal God even as we move. You have to be careful how you move because every movement you make ought to be a movement of worship. Everything we do has to bring Him glory, because we were made to make Him happy.

When you remember that you were made for God's pleasure, that thought will stop you from doing worldly things. For example, every time you are tempted to take that drink, just say, "I was made to make Him happy." See if you can still drink that glass of vodka while you are giving God glory and telling Him how worthy He is; you can't do it. That's why worship will keep you out of the world, and the world will keep you from worshiping.

> Worship will keep you out of the world—and the world will keep you from worshiping.

The Worship of God Takes Precedence

Again, God wants us to understand that we were made to worship Him. Now, we have the ability to worship anything, to show the worth of anything. You can rightfully show the worth of your wife, and in that sense worth-ship her, by dressing her up and making her the admiration of every man when she walks through the door; you can enhance her, magnify her, send her to the beauty shop, pay for that hairdo if you have to, and make her look just like a queen.

You can show worth-ship to your children. You can demonstrate their value to you by believing that they are worth putting through college, by buying them things that will bless them, and by teaching them principles that you know will lift them up.

You can show worth-ship to your old house by fixing it up: cleaning it, waxing the floors, adding awnings and window coverings, laying down new carpet, and bringing the termite inspector in to get rid of those creatures that are not paying rent.

You can show worth-ship to your car by washing it so that no one has to keep writing "wash me" on it, and by getting new tires so you're not riding around on bald eagles. That's showing worth-ship.

But the bottom line is, Exodus 20:3 says, *"You shall have no other* [little] *gods before Me."* God didn't say you can't have things; He said, "Just don't put any of these things before Me." You can show the worth-ship of things, such as I just mentioned, but *God's* worth-ship— His worthiness—supersedes, overrides, takes precedence over anything and everything else. You have to keep things in perspective so that you don't make God jealous, because He is a jealous God (Exodus 34:14). If you're not careful and you put things or people before Him, He'll knock down their place in your life, like He did the false god Dagon. (See 1 Samuel 5:1–4.) He will not have any other gods before Him.

A God of Ardor and Order

Our God is a God of *ardor* (passion) as well as a God of *order* (organization). He wants us to understand Him as a God of passion and zeal. That is how many of us know Him. God is an awesome God; He reins. Our God is a consuming fire. Our God is terrible; He is a man of war; His right hand and His holy arm have gotten Him the victory. Yes, God is like that, but He is also very orderly.

So, by the same token, when He sees us coming to Him, He says, "I don't want you just to be full of zeal; I don't want you to have all this passion and no knowledge. I want you to know Me, for *'the people who know their God shall be strong, and carry out great exploits'* (Daniel 11:32)." Knowing God as He reveals Himself in the Word keeps us orderly as we worship Him. Then we are worshiping him in both spirit and truth.

When I say that God wants us to know Him, I mean that He wants us to know Him in the sense of being intimately acquainted with Him. We are not just to know His actions or His thoughts; we also need to know His ways. Now, knowing His ways is going to require that we go deeper than having mere head knowledge of the Word of God.

The Tabernacle: A Pattern for Worship

The Bible says, *"Sanctify them by Your truth. Your word is truth"* (John 17:17). The Word of the Lord, or the Word of Truth, gives us the principles whereby we are to come to God and know Him in an intimate way. It teaches us that we just don't go popping in on God, saying, "Hey, God, how are You doing today? Thought I'd come in and say 'Hey.' Let's sit around and just talk awhile." No. In the Old Testament, and also in the New

Testament, there is a pattern for worship, so that the ardor of God and the order of God come together in our lives.

The pattern for worship is found in the tabernacle of Moses, a kind of portable sanctuary prescribed by God (see Exodus 25–31) and used by the Israelites when they were wandering in the wilderness for forty years. This was the place where God met with the children of Israel. The Levites carried the tabernacle wherever the Israelites traveled throughout that wilderness.

The tabernacle represented the pattern that God gave the Israelites in order for them to come to Him and worship Him. Exodus 25:9 says, *"According to all that I show thee, after the pattern of the tabernacle, and the pattern of all the instruments thereof, even so shall ye make it"* (KJV). From the outer court through the Holy Place, and all the way into the Holy of Holies, you will find that God set forth a pattern for worship. This pattern is symbolized by the tabernacle furniture: the bronze altar, the laver, the lampstand, the table of showbread, the altar of incense, and the ark of the covenant.

Many of us have already experienced the ardor of the Lord as we've worshiped Him. Right now we're going to talk about His order, so that we can worship Him in both spirit and truth.

The Principle of "Three"

The tabernacle was established as a model for worship based upon the principle of the number three. It was made up of three areas: the outer court; the inner court, called the Holy Place; and the Most Holy Place, also called the Holy of Holies. The Father, the Son, and the Holy Spirit are symbolically represented in the tabernacle. Jesus' designation as the Way, the Truth, and the Life is symbolically represented there. The kingdom, the power, and the glory are also represented in this glorious tabernacle. God is going to use all of this imagery to bring us into an understanding of true worship.

Let me just say a word or two about the significance of the number three. The number three is an important number both in Scripture and in men's dealings with the world. First of all, the number three represents a dimensional God of height, breadth, and length. It represents what is solid; what is whole; what is substantial; what is real, complete, and entire.

God uses the number three to teach us the principle of wholeness. Through this principle, we learn that we cannot take just part of Him. We cannot take just the part of Him that makes us "happy." We're going to have to deal with every part of Him, touch all of the bases, if we're going to get all that He has for us. There are no shortcuts; we have to go through a process of growing and maturing. As I like to say,

"You don't lie down a blunder and wake up a wonder."

"You don't lie down a blunder and wake up a wonder" in the kingdom of God. God wants us to recognize that if we're going to come to Him, we're going to have to come in His order, according to His plan. That's how He dealt with Israel, and we're no exception.

There are many themes and concepts that are grouped in threes; this enables us to have a better understanding of them. For example, there are three main attributes of God—His omniscience, His omnipresence, and His omnipotence. The three capabilities of man are thought, word, and deed. When we discuss degrees or make comparisons, we talk about good, better, and best.

However, the highest grouping of three is the Father, the Son, and the Holy Spirit. When you really start looking at what God wants for you in regard to your spiritual growth, you will see that you must think in terms of the *fullness* of God. You have to have a relationship with God the Father, God the Son, and God the Holy Spirit. You need to receive everything you can from the Lord.

The Outer Court

The Bronze Altar Represents Christ's Blood

It is significant for our understanding of the tabernacle that it was made up of three areas. Again, these areas were the outer court; the inner court, called the Holy Place; and the Most Holy Place, also called the Holy of Holies.

When you look at the tabernacle of Moses, one of the first things you see is the outer court. In the outer court there is a bronze altar—there it is, staring you right in the face. You can't go any further because it represents the blood of the sacrifice. It represents dealing with sin. The bronze altar reminds us that we cannot have a relationship with God without dealing with sin. We cannot worship God without dealing with sin—and dealing with sin means that we have to come to God through Jesus, who shed His blood on the cross. No one can worship God who has not been saved by the power of the blood. He will not give you access to Himself otherwise. You can try; you can go through all of the gyrations; you can jump up, spin around three times, fall down on your knees, and prostrate yourself, but it won't work until you become a child of God.

The children of God have access; we have access through Christ's blood. *"According to the law almost all things are purified with blood, and without shedding of blood there is no remission* [forgiveness of sin]*"* (Hebrews 9:22). We can't draw near to God unless we come by the blood. Thank God for the blood. Thank God for the cross. Thank God for Calvary, because it deals with the penalty of sin. Thank God for Jesus!

The Laver Represents the Cleansing of the Word

When you move past the bronze altar and are able to say, "I have peace with God through the blood of the Lord Jesus Christ" (see Colossians 1:20), the next thing you see in front of you is the bronze laver. The laver of the tabernacle was a large bowl used for purification, and it represents the washing of the water of the Word. (See Ephesians 5:25–26.) There are those who try to worship God in spirit and in truth, but they have not been cleansed by the truth of God's Word, and so they offer up praise out of their fleshly nature. They end up giving Him tainted praise; they end up giving Him praise that is unacceptable. (See Leviticus 10:1–2 KJV.)

The outer court of the tabernacle represents God the Father: who He is, what He has done, and what He offers His people. The court was used for public worship; it was where the people gave praise to God. It was also the place where they offered sacrifices. Therefore, in the outer court, spiritually speaking, we're going to be singing songs to and about God. These need to be offered in spirit and in truth, after we have been cleansed by His Word.

In this sense, the outer court also represents the sacrifice of praise that we give Him as we enter into His gates with thanksgiving. As we enter the outer court, we celebrate our salvation. We are able to sing hymns, and we are able to celebrate everything that God has done for us. We offer testimonies telling what He has given us; we sing songs about the blood of Jesus. We clap our hands, use tambourines, and dance to celebrate our deliverance. Through our praise, we tell our fleshly nature, "I'm not going to let you have authority over me."

Now, even though we are to enter into His gates with thanksgiving and come into His courts with praise (Psalm 100:4), there are many people who come in with a whole lot of things other than praise and thanksgiving. So God has a way of gathering our thoughts and emotions unto Him. He does it by cleansing us through the washing of the water of the Word so that we can offer Him our purest praise.

The laver, which represents the place and instrument of cleansing, was made out of bronze mirrors given by the women who served at the entrance to the tabernacle. We can draw much significance from this, because God wants us to see ourselves as we come to meet with Him. When we look into the mirror of His Word, it gives us a chance to see ourselves as we really are and be purified. When we enter into His gates, if there is unforgiveness, if there is malice, if there are all kinds of strange spirits that we've been dealing with during the week, the Word of the Lord is there to cleanse us before we dare to enter into His presence.

> God wants us to see ourselves as we come to meet with Him.

The Outer Curtain Represents Access to God

The outer court and the inner court, or Holy Place, of the Tabernacle were separated by a curtained entrance, which symbolically represents our flesh. When we offer pure praise to God, we gain access to Him (we enter through the curtain, so to speak) so that we might give Him glory and honor.

We need to reach the place where we can push past this curtain through our pure and genuine praise. We need to push past attitudes, such as the following: "I'm tired." "I don't feel like praising God." "I stood in line too long." "Why do we have to go through this?" "I don't want to go to this service." "Why do we have to sing this song?" When we are able to push past these types of feelings and attitudes, we're pushing past the curtained entrance. We purpose in our hearts to praise God, saying, "*I will bless the LORD at all times*' (Psalm 34:1). I don't feel like it, but I'm going to bless Him anyway. I don't know exactly what's going to happen, and I don't know why I had to go through what I had to go through to get here, but now that I am here, I'm going to bless Him."

Sometimes, when we begin to bless Him, we do so nonchalantly. While the choir is singing, while the praise team is praising and worshiping, we're sitting there trying to remember, "Did I turn the stove off or didn't I?" or "Why did Johnny say that to me on the way to church?" or "Why did she call me right as I was walking out the door?" And God is saying, "I'm trying to get your attention. I'm trying to bring you into a place where you can enjoy My presence."

Now, when He finally gets some of your attention, and you raise your hands to Him a little bit and say, "All right, all right, I'll bless Him," as strange as it may seem, that's enough for a beginning. God has gotten your attention; He has started you on your way into His presence, even with that slight lifting of your hands to Him. "Well," you continue, "I don't feel like it, but all right. The preacher is telling me to praise the Lord; the worship leader is telling me to say 'Hallelujah,' and so I will."

God starts you on the path to praising Him, and then He takes you and begins to draw you, by His loving-kindness and tender mercy, into a place where you will give Him more. By giving Him more, you will receive more and, in turn, give more. As you continue to focus your thoughts on God, while obeying the Word and truly entering into the praises of God's people, you will push through the curtain. Then you might do things others consider crazy, as an expression of your worship. You might twirl around; you might dance or skip. You might even leap or run! That's when you become hilariously foolish about praising your God. At this point, God has you. Now He can bring you all the way into Himself.

The bronze altar and laver show us that a child of God initially comes to Him by way of the blood of Jesus, and then lets the Word sanctify his heart for worship. So push past your flesh and come into a place where you can focus on Jesus, because the next room, the Holy Place, is all about Jesus. Remember that the outer court is about God the Father: His loving-kindness, His tender mercy, His faithfulness, what He is able to do, and what He's already done. In the outer court, you can testify to everybody that our God is an awesome God. You can tell them that He is a faithful God, that great is His faithfulness, for He has saved and preserved your life.

Push past your flesh and come into a place where you can focus on Jesus.

The Holy Place

We can see, then, how genuine praise to God moves us from the outer court to the Holy Place. In the Holy Place we see God the Son depicted in various pieces of furniture: the lampstand, the table of showbread, and the altar of incense.

The Lampstand Represents the Filling of the Spirit

Since the tabernacle and its furnishings are the pattern for our worship, God is telling us that, at a certain

91

point, when we enter the Holy Place, we're going to be face-to-face with the lampstand. The lampstand represents Jesus as the Vine and us as the branches. (See John 15:5.) It represents the exalted name of Jesus. It represents Jesus as the Light of the World. It represents the warmth of the Holy Spirit, and it represents the pouring of the oil of gladness into our lives. God wants you to experience all of these things as you prepare to fully touch Him with your spirit and worship Him in the Holy of Holies.

To use our ongoing analogy of intimacy between a husband and wife, this is like foreplay that precedes intercourse. In natural lovemaking, it shouldn't be "slam-bam, thank you, ma'am," and I can imagine Jesus saying, "Don't give Me 'slam-bam, thank you, ma'am,' either. I gave My life for you. Give Me some foreplay; give Me some attention. Give Me some praise! Come, bask in My holy presence."

I hear Him continue to say, "I want you to know that I love attention and that I love for you to let Me know how you feel about Me." So when you come into the Holy Place, you should be paying attention to Jesus, and saying, "I love You, Jesus. Thank You, Lord. You've been good to me. There is no greater name I know; bless the wonderful name of Jesus." You should be enjoying His presence, loving Him for who He is.

You will also be walking in the light, because Jesus is the Light of the World. In addition, you will receive a better understanding of the Bible, as God's Word is illuminated to you. As you praise the name of Jesus, the Spirit of the living God will start welling up inside you, until He fills you up. And as you are being filled with the Spirit, you will be experiencing the fullness of God, right there at the lampstand.

Through the fellowship that we experience with God in the outer court, at the bronze altar, we enter into *sonship* as a child of God. When we come to the laver, we enter into *discipleship,* the studying of the Word of God. And when we come to the lampstand, we receive *stewardship,* because the power and authority of the name of Jesus, along with the gifts of the Spirit, are released, and we have to know how to handle them in the proper way. We have to walk in love and operate under spiritual authority, so that we can maintain order in worship.

The Table of Showbread Represents Fellowship

After we experience Jesus at the lampstand, we find Him also at the table of showbread, because He is our source of *fellowship.* He is the common denominator that brings all believers together by His Spirit.

When you are truly filled with His Spirit, you want to have fellowship with other believers. As you walk across the inner court from the lampstand to the table of showbread, you will see other believers who also are filled with the same Spirit. It is here that you will realize you're not the only pebble on the beach; you're not the only star in the sky. You have been filled with the Holy Spirit and have been given gifts, but you will discover that your brothers and sisters have, too, and you will desire to fellowship with them. *"If we walk in the light as He is in the light, we have fellowship with one another, and the blood of Jesus Christ His Son cleanses us from all sin"* (1 John 1:7).

When you are truly filled with the Spirit, you want to have fellowship with other believers.

Nothing else could bring us together but Jesus. Nobody else could bring us together but Jesus. No other name could bring us together but the name of Jesus. Mohammed won't work, Buddha is dead, and Confucius was confused. Only Jesus, who is the Head of the church (see Ephesians 5:23), can bring us together. Jesus, the Showbread, is our common denominator.

Some Christians may not dress as we do, but they've got Jesus; some may not talk as we do, but they've got Jesus; some may not live in our neighborhoods, but they've got Jesus; they may not go to our schools, but they've got Jesus; they may not drive our kind of car, but they've got Jesus. And if they've got Jesus, we can have fellowship! He is our common denominator. He is the Bread of Life. There is Bread on the table of showbread, and the same Bread that we eat is the Bread that they eat. Jesus, and only Jesus, can bring us together.

God prepares us as He fills us with His Spirit, and then He lends us to each other in a time of fellowship at the table of showbread. When all of us come to the table, we see each one as being just as important as everybody else. At the table of showbread, there are no big "I"s or little "you"s. We should be able to submit ourselves one to another (Ephesians 5:21).

This is important, because the Word of God says that while we're *"submitting to one another in the fear of God"* (v. 21), and as we are filled with His Spirit, we will begin to sing *"psalms and hymns and spiritual songs"* (v. 19). Psalms are songs based upon the Word. Hymns, for the most part, are born out of testimonies. Spiritual songs are given directly from God to our spirits. All of them are important to our worship. But starting in the outer court, some of us need to learn the hymns of the church, because there is a great joy that goes along with singing hymns, particularly hymns about the blood of Christ. They remind us of Calvary and take us back to the time when we first met the Lord. This stirs us, because nothing can compare to the power of the blood in our lives.

As we sing hymns in the outer court, if we love the Lord at all, a passion for Him is aroused in us, and something happens that breaks through our stony hearts and overrides our fleshly nature. (See Ezekiel 11:19.) Special moments of intimacy occur between us and the Lord, which free us to sing Word songs, the psalms of the ages, and songs about Jesus in the Holy Place.

Every part of our progression into the Holy of Holies is important to God. Why? He wants us to get every bit of Him, because it cost Him everything to open to us the Way, the Truth, and the Life. He opened the way at the bronze altar (Calvary). His Word was given to us so that we might have truth (John 17:17) and life (John 20:31). And then, when we came into the Holy Place, He showed us who the Way is, and the Way is Jesus. *"I am the way, the truth, and the life. No one comes to the Father except through Me"* (John 14:6).

The Altar of Incense Represents Intercession

When we get to the altar of incense, we are moving a little closer to the pure presence of the Lord. We are coming into a place where we can start to feel what the Lord feels, even before we see Him face-to-face. We are touched by what touches Him. Through the language of worship, we are showing Him what He is really worth.

The altar of incense was where the priest ministered in the tabernacle. It was the place of intercession. At the altar of incense, we move beyond the place where we are merely lifting or waving our hands to God in praise. When we see Jesus at the lampstand and know that the oil in the lamp came from His being crushed for our sins, it will bring tears to our eyes. As we remember the great things He's done for us, and the fellowship we now have with the Father and other believers through His exalted name, an overwhelming desire for others to experience His blessings will cause us to pray for them. This is called intercession. To me, this word means that we have "entered the session" of prayer being conducted by our Savior, and we can agree with Him as He continues in prayer for us. (See Hebrews 7:25.) Now we are on our way to...

...Entering the Holy of Holies

Chapter Six
Entering the Holy of Holies

O ur ascent into the presence of the Lord in the Holy of Holies is a progressive one. At the lampstand, we are filled with His Spirit and a greater understanding of His power. Then, when we see Jesus at the table of showbread, we experience fellowship with Him and other believers.

Here, Jesus gives us His love for others. He is the Vine and we are branches. When we abide in Him, His love abides in us. I may not even know someone, but Jesus gives me a love that lets me look at him or her through His eyes. He gives His followers this love because it is by *love* that all men will know that we are His disciples (John 13:34–35).

Called to Love

This means that we must love each other before we can truly love Him. So before I discuss being in the presence of God in the Holy of Holies, I want to talk for a moment about the importance of loving others. We often have the idea that we're going to be able to sit over in a corner and worship God in spirit and in truth all by ourselves. To some extent, this is true. Before we get to that point, however, we have to be able to deal with others. How can you say you love God whom you have not seen when you hate your brother whom you see every day? (1 John 4:20). How are you going to worship God when you have an attitude about somebody you're sitting next to? The Bible teaches us that if we're going to love God, we have to love His children, too.

When we love one another, there is a flow of love from heart to heart. When God gives us His love, we have to give it to others; we have to get it inside them. If they look as though they don't want to have anything to do with you, you've got to work extra hard, because it's your job to get the love inside them. Get it to them; get it into them; go ahead and encourage them with the love of God. When they're looking stone-faced, exhort them with the love of God. When they're looking all mean, bless them with the love of God. Smile until you get them to smile back. Love everyone until you are sure they have received it. That's what we're called to do.

We are called to be in fellowship with one another. In fellowship, there is "more than one fellow in the ship." That means everybody in the ship should be able to feel your love. We have to touch as many folks as we can in the ship. *Let us do good to all, especially to those who are of the household of faith*" (Galatians 6:10).

Wherever we are right now is our mission field, and love is our mission.

Some people think they want to become missionaries, but they don't love the people where they are right now. Wherever we are right now is our mission field, *and love is our mission.*

I think you understand what I'm trying to say. When we're walking together and are fellowshipping with one another, and fellowshipping with Him, then the call to love is not so hard to answer. Then, and only then, can we truly answer the high call of intercession! (See Philippians 3:14.)

100

Called to Be Intercessors

"Wherefore he is able also to save them to the uttermost that come unto God by him, seeing he ever liveth to make intercession for them" (Hebrews 7:25 KJV). Jesus is always praying for us, and we are to be just like Him. We are called to be intercessors. We are called to *"stand in the gap"* (Ezekiel 22:30) for others. He doesn't call us just to get happy and then to go out and pass by somebody who is still suffering, or who has not yet found Him, or who is not in the place where we are, and say, "I'm so glad I'm not like her." But our assignment is to pray, to stand in the gap, and to touch God concerning others until they become just like Him. And in praying for others, we become more like Him, too. People need prayer, and we need to be perfected through the practice of praying for others.

God is calling us now, as the kings and priests that we are (Revelation 1:6), to stand in the gap. As we stand in the gap and pray earnestly, more often than not, we will experience the presence of the Lord. Can God trust us to talk to Him about the needs of others? Can God trust us to bear one another's burdens? Can God trust us to pray for our leaders? If He can, He will saturate us with His presence and answer our prayers.

> Your praise will be empty if your prayer life is not full.

You can praise all you want, but if you offer praise without prayer, you're not going to get all you desire from the Lord. There is no power without prayer. Your praise will be empty if your prayer life is not full.

Intercession requires a certain attitude. You have to be willing to travail. When a woman is in labor, she has to be ready to push until the baby is finally born. Likewise, we have to be ready to push spiritually. In other words, we will have to *p-u-s-h,* that is, **pray until something happens!** We have been called to push because many people may not have anyone but us to travail on their behalf. To be effective intercessors, we always have to be ready to pray.

We should pray in agreement with His Word, because when we do, God answers our prayers and teaches us even more how to pray for others. As Jesus said, pray in this manner: *"Our Father which art in heaven, hallowed* [holy] *be thy name. Thy kingdom come. Thy will be done in earth, as it is in heaven"* (Matthew 6:9–10 KJV). We need to pray, "Lord, I want Your reign to rule over me and all the earth." When we stand in the gap as priests unto God, somebody's life is going to be changed! And if you get to a point where you don't know what to pray for as you ought (Romans 8:26), that's when the Holy Spirit's intercession will begin.

Now, the Holy Spirit does know how to pray according to God's will, and when the Spirit of the Lord is invoked in prayer, God enables us to break past the second veil of our emotions and our minds. Then, as our spirits and God's Spirit unite, we will slip into the Holy of Holies and experience true intimacy as only God can give it.

A New and Living Way

In this place we will receive the ministry of God the Spirit, because the Spirit of the Lord gives life (2 Corinthians 3:6). So we move past the second curtain and into the Holy of Holies, to experience our God as the Life-giver.

Now, in the days of Moses, only the high priest could go all the way into the presence of God in the Holy of Holies. I'm so glad this is not Moses' day, because, when Jesus, the Son of God, came, He came to make this pattern of the tabernacle come alive for us. He consecrated a *"new and living way"* through the curtain, that is, His body. This truth is found in Hebrews 10:20. In fact, chapters nine and ten of Hebrews talk about Jesus as our sacrificial offering and our High Priest. What a revelation!

Jesus provided a new and living way into the Holy of Holies through His body and His blood. Now He has left the gate open for us. He declared Himself to be the Door, saying that if we would come in by Him, we would be saved. We would go in and out, and we would find pasture (John 10:9). Jesus is the only access to the Father in heaven. This is true both in salvation and in worship. If we are going to worship God, we are going to have to come by Jesus Christ. He is the Door. He is the Gate. He is the Way, the Truth, and the Life. This means that, if we are going to get to God the Father, we are going to have to reach Him by Jesus. No one else will do. You can scratch everybody else off your list.

> Jesus is the only access to the Father in heaven.

We can see that Jesus is the way to God through all the symbolism of the tabernacle. Through His life, and even in His death, He walked through the tabernacle, fulfilling its pattern completely. When He sacrificed His life on the cross, He was our burnt offering and sin offering on the bronze altar in the outer court.

He not only was the offering on the *bronze altar,* but He was also the *water in the laver.* He is the Water of Life. He is the Living Water. *"Whoever drinks of the water that I shall give him will never thirst"* (John 4:14).

In addition, He is the Word that shows us ourselves as a mirror. And, at the same time that He shows us ourselves, He cleanses us. He washes us by the water of the Word so that He can present us as a glorious church

(Ephesians 5:27). He was the Sanctified One. *"I sanctify Myself"* (John 17:19), Jesus said. And He was the Sanctifier. "I have sanctified those whom You have given Me. I have lost none of them," He said. (See verse 12.)

Jesus was also the *center stem of the lampstand.* To incorporate another biblical analogy, He is the Vine that lets us connect to Him as branches, so that we might be filled with the Holy Spirit and receive the gifts of the Spirit. He is the lampstand itself. He is the Light of the World, so that we also might be the light of the world. *"You are the light of the world. A city that is set on a hill cannot be hidden"* (Matthew 5:14).

He is the Great High Priest at the altar of incense, who prays for us.

> *But this man, because he continueth ever, hath an unchangeable priesthood. Wherefore he is able also to save them to the uttermost that come unto God by him, seeing he ever liveth to make intercession for them.* (Hebrews 7:24–25 KJV)

He is not only the Great High Priest, but also the curtain, or *veil*—the second curtain that separated the Holy Place from the Holy of Holies. He was the curtain that was torn in two in order to give us access to God. (See Matthew 27:50–51.) He was bruised and broken, cursed and chastised, pierced and punished for our sake. *"He was wounded for our transgressions, He was bruised for our iniquities; the chastisement for our peace was upon Him, and by His stripes we are healed"* (Isaiah 53:5). He did all of this. *"He made Him who knew no sin to be sin for us, that we might become the righteousness of God in Him"* (2 Corinthians 5:21). He allowed Himself to be crucified. He laid down His own life, saying, *"No one takes [My life] from Me, but I lay it down of Myself. I have power to lay it down, and I have power to take it again"* (John 10:18), and

"Destroy this temple, and in three days I will raise it up" (John 2:19).

All of the prophecies about Him were fulfilled. He said, *"And I, if I am lifted up from the earth, will draw all peoples to Myself"* (John 12:32). He talked about Himself, and then He made good on His promises. He did all of this so that He might give us access to the Father. He opened the gate wide for *"whosover will"* (Revelation 22:17) to come!

Given all this, are you going to be lazy and not go all the way in unto Him—after all that He has done, after all that He has given, after all that He has become, just so you could have access to the Father? He did this for you so that you wouldn't have to go to a priest and say, "Would you please go to God for me? Would you please pray for me? Would you please talk to the Man Upstairs for me?" Instead, you can talk to Him yourself. God, through Christ, has given us the opportunity to come into His presence. We can *"come boldly to the throne of grace, that we may obtain mercy and find grace to help in time of need"* (Hebrews 4:16). And we do have many needs.

> Given all that Jesus has done, are we going to be lazy and not go all the way in unto Him?

Now Jesus has sat down *"at the right hand of the throne of God"* (Hebrews 12:2). *"And we beheld His glory, the glory as of the only begotten of the Father, full of grace and truth"* (John 1:14). As our continual Priest, He is never going to die, and *"He always lives to make intercession for* [us]*"* (Hebrews 7:25). Let me repeat that God now gives us the opportunity to go beyond the curtain and into His presence in the Holy of Holies as we are praying and praising, so that we can experience intimacy, and so that we can experience the glory of God resting upon us.

105

The Ark of the Covenant

The glory, or *Shechinah,* of God, rested in the Holy of Holies in the tabernacle. Today His glory is in us as believers. The Holy Place contained the lampstand, the table of showbread, and the altar of incense. In the Holy of Holies, however, there was only one piece of furniture: the ark of the covenant. It was symbolic of the presence of the Lord.

Seed Time

Now, beloved, when we are in the true presence of the Lord, we receive from Him in a way that we could not otherwise. When we reach this place, we are no longer just going to sing songs *about* God; we are no longer just going to sing songs *to* Him; we will have opportunity to sing songs that come *from* Him! He will give us something that we didn't come in with. He will give us a song we have never heard before. Jesus is ready to send us out to minister in His name, but before He can send us out, we have to experience "seed time."

I know we often think of "seed time" as a time when we give our money, but that's "sowing time." Seed time is the time when God deposits things in you, and He deposits things in you in times of worship. Seed time is when He puts something in the ground of your heart that has to first die in order to bring forth fruit (John 12:24). Seed time is what happens when you're worshiping God, and God shows you who you are, and starts killing off what is not from Him. In His presence, His consuming fire starts burning away things that you and I thought we would never be able to let go of. That's what happens when you're worshiping.

God calls us in to worship, and He renovates us with His refining fire before giving us more seed. (See Malachi

3:3.) God wants to set us on fire, not just so that we will run around the building, but so that we will walk straight when our feet hit the ground.

We saw earlier that we cannot have a relationship with God without dealing with sin. Just as we can't enter into worship when we're angry or bitter, there is no place for these things when we're in the midst of pure, intimate worship. In fact, hatred, bitterness, and fear will flee away in the true presence of God.

Take it from me, when you have been in the presence of God, it will be much easier to treat everybody right. The fruit of the Spirit will be evident. You won't be able to look at somebody cross-eyed when you've been worshiping. You won't be able to tell anybody off after you've been worshiping; you won't be able to give anybody a piece of your mind. Others might try to give you a piece of their mind, but you won't be affected by it. You'll be so caught up in God that it won't provoke you. We need to be able to tell God, "I want Your seed, so bring on the fire!"

Fullness of Joy

Every worship experience ought to kill off something and birth something new in us. After God deposits revelation; after He deposits His seed, and we die a little, we come out of worship with joy. We go forth with peace. The mountains and the hills—the troubles we were facing before—will just break forth before us. (See Isaiah 55:12.) They won't look as big as they used to, because He is magnified above everything else. Not only will the mountains and hills break forth before us, but also the trees of the field, the trees of righteousness, are going to clap their hands as we go out with joy (v. 12). In the timing of the Lord, some of those trees don't yet know they are trees of righteousness. They are still out snorting and cavorting. But they are going to clap their hands as you and I go out with joy. I don't mean that we will go out just having had a good time, but in His presence there is *"fullness of joy"* (Psalm 16:11), and joy overrides circumstances.

Joy will override our situations. Joy is the fruit of a moment of intimacy we have with Jesus that lasts for a lifetime. If you will just rewind the tape of your life, I'm

> Joy is the fruit of a moment of intimacy we have with Jesus that lasts for a lifetime.

sure you can remember times you've had with the Lord that you'll never forget. I know I have. These are times that cannot be explained away. Every time you think about them, you have joy. You will never be the same because of them. It

doesn't matter if you've just lost your job; I dare you to think about something you have experienced in the presence of the Lord; it will bring you joy. God's joy is *"inexpressible and full of glory"* (1 Peter 1:8).

Now, when we start out at the bronze altar and the laver, we are forgiven and cleansed, and we come into the kingdom. When we go into the Holy Place, we experience the power of praise and the power of the Holy Spirit. But when we go beyond the second curtain and into God's presence, spirit-to-Spirit, there's nothing but glory. When we are really worshiping, we can't say anything about God but glory. We can't tell God how we feel about someone who has wronged us. We can't tell God how we want this and that. We are only able to say, "Glory, glory to You, Lord, because You're worthy."

There is glory that God wants us to experience. There is glory prepared for us if we will come in His way and not try to sidestep Him or shortcut the process or try to bombard our way on in. We need to follow the pattern of worship. Come in raising your hands. However, when you really get into His presence, you will probably just bow. Like me, you won't be able to stand. You won't have any strength. You will need His seed. But when you come out of His presence, use the power He gives!

Power through His Presence

When we come all the way past the second curtain and are worshiping and touching Him spirit-to-Spirit, then God infuses us with strength and with joy. He infuses us with complete confidence in Him, so that we can believe God for anything and everything while we are worshiping. It doesn't matter what the devil told you; it doesn't matter what he tried to do. When you get into the presence of the Lord and start worshiping, you feel as if you can run through a troop and leap over a wall (2 Samuel 22:30); you feel as if you are able to leap tall buildings in a single bound; you feel more powerful than a locomotive, faster than a speeding bullet. You are prepared for warfare. This is what true worship does for the believer.

A Change of Attitude

The Lord says that when you know the truth, the truth makes you free, and you are no longer bound (John 8:32). God's Word is truth (John 17:17), and His truth shows us how God gives us access to Himself. The Word of God shows us how Christ fulfilled the pattern of the tabernacle and gave us access to the Holy of Holies. Jesus came all the way through to the Holy of Holies, and you also can come all the way through, because He's left the gate open. The Word says, *"As He is, so are we in this world"* (1 John 4:17).

What we have available to us right now can't help but affect our attitudes. If we really understand all that God has done for us, if we look at the tabernacle of Moses and allow God to unfold to us the truth in it—the meticulous way that He allowed His Son to be offered for us, to be a pattern for us, to be a way for us—we will get to the place where we're no longer complacent. We can no longer "take it or leave it"; we have to have His fullness. We will recognize that it cost God too much for us to act as if what He did for us doesn't mean anything. And so, as we learn the truth, and as we grow in grace and in the knowledge of the Lord Jesus Christ (2 Peter 3:18), our attitudes, our spirits, our motives concerning worship will change. Our desire to show the worth-ship of our God will increase to the point that we don't mind doing whatever it takes to *"make His praise glorious"* (Psalm 66:2)!

I've learned that if you stop and think long enough, you can always find something to be thankful for. God is looking for somebody who is thankful. He is looking for somebody who will bless His name, someone who will make His praise glorious. We do that by telling Him about His name. Tell Him what His name has done; tell Him what His name means to you; tell Him how powerful His name is; tell Him how sweet His name is. Boast about what happens when you call on His name. Tell Him. Even though your praise can't get as high as His name, keep getting on your tiptoes and trying. Keep on praising, because the Lord is worthy, and you're showing His worth-ship every time you magnify His name.

Practice singing, even if you can't carry a tune. Sing just because you have a heart to; sing because you're

You're showing His worth-ship every time you magnify His name.

happy; sing because you're free. If nobody else wants to listen to you, it doesn't matter, because you are not singing to them, anyway. *"Make a joyful noise unto the LORD"* (Psalm 98:4 KJV); sing to the Lord, because this will get you ready to embrace the truth found in the seed of His Word. This is the spirit of true worship.

Come Out Singing

And when we come out of the presence of the Lord after we have been worshiping, we come out singing, we come out shouting, and nobody can doubt that we have been with Jesus. We come out ready for warfare and witnessing. We come out clapping our hands and applauding Him because He's been so good. God is so good. He, and He alone, satisfies!

When God touches a certain spot in me, I just lose it. Oh, He knows how to touch us; He knows how to satisfy. And when we as the church are in His presence, being touched by Him, we sing corporate songs that strengthen us as a body. We should never walk out on worship before it's over, because we never know when the moment of climax will come.

When we do go out, however, we go out to bring others back with us. Something has been birthed in our hearts that says, "Lord, others need what I have received from You. You're big enough to give to all who come to You. Your breasts are full; there is enough milk for me and for everybody else. I don't have to be selfish. I want to go and bring others back."

How do we bring others back? Jesus says, "Tell them about Me. Tell them that I love them. Tell them the Good News concerning Me." (See Matthew 28:18–20.) Worship opens the door for us to witness and invite others to come to Him.

Come to Jesus

Here is what I share with those who do not yet know Jesus:

"Jesus is there with you when you go to worship. He knows what you're feeling; He knows what you need; He's ready to give to you. Jesus knows all, because He became Man and experienced what we experience. He walked on earth; He struggled; He was *'despised and rejected'* (Isaiah 53:3).

"If you do not know Him but want to know Him, the first step is to come to the outer court, to come to the bronze altar where the blood has been shed for you. I urge you to come to Him; you know that you need Him. Hallelujah! He's been waiting for you. The blood has been shed for you. Don't you know that Jesus knows all about you and your struggles? He knows.

"Jesus said, *'Wide is the gate and broad is the way that leads to destruction, and there are many who go in by it'* (Matthew 7:13). So if you want to worship God, but don't know Him, you need to follow the pattern for worship that we have been talking about. Come by the cross; come and receive the blood that has been shed on your account; it's been placed on the mercy seat.

To worship God, you must come by way of the cross.

"Won't you say yes to the Lord? Come on, He's waiting for you; you need to come. There are just a few who are going to be able to find the way, even though He *is* the Way. Jesus is the Way. He knows you; He guided you to me so that you could know the way to Him. Do you know that 'He will guide till the day is done'? There is no friend like Jesus. You need to know Him; press your way into the presence of the Lord.

"Our worship experience is a choice that we make. Jesus says, 'Come in through the gate.' And when you come through the gate, don't look for bulls and goats, the kinds of sacrifices the Israelites used to have to make. We no longer have to offer them, for the blood of Jesus has been shed once and for all on our behalf. Jesus says to us, 'Come just as you are. Bring yourself as an offering, and let Me work on you and prepare you to be a sanctuary, one who will give Me glory and honor, one whom I can trust to enter into a full relationship with Me.' Thank Him for the blood. No worship experience is complete until you thank Him for the blood. Thank Him that He saved you.

"Remember that you cannot experience or enjoy worship apart from the Word; it is the truth that lends substantiation to what we do and why we do it.

"There is life waiting for you. The pattern of worship that we've been talking about is what He wants you to experience as you press your way, singing about Him, singing to Him, and then letting Him sing to you.

"Start now by entering into the outer court, singing to Him, 'Come into my heart, Lord Jesus.' Let Him hear you sing. Say to Him, 'I need You, Lord. I call upon Your name. God, I receive your Son, Jesus.' Lift high your voice. Let Him into your heart today, because *'now is the day of salvation'* (2 Corinthians 6:2)."

This is the witness that I would share with one who does not know the Lord. We must be ready, as we come out of true worship, to give the kind of genuine witness that will help someone else come to Christ.

True worship will also enable us to enter into a deeper relationship with the Lord ourselves. When we do this, we will come into His presence...

...Anointing the Lord

Chapter Seven

Anointing the Lord

We have to fall in love with God. We fall in love with other people, and they often don't even know what real love is. God is looking for someone who will fall in love with Him. We're to love Him so much that we are glad just to be able to express our love. To fall in love with Him as our Savior is the first thing we ought to be able to do. Nobody but nobody could have done for us what He did in raising us from the dunghill of life.

The *pattern* of worship, which we talked about in the last two chapters, and through which we come into the presence of God, prepares us for the *posture* of worship. God wants us to anoint Him. He wants us to pour honor upon Him as a reflection of our love. There are three postures of honor that we need to show Him in order to experience Him in His fullness. Jesus was anointed three times when He lived and walked among men: as Prophet, as Priest, and as King. These anointings are symbolic of the three postures of worship, because they represent three ways in which we are to approach and relate to God: 1) with repentance, 2) with service permeated with worship, and 3) with a life committed to His Lordship. In this chapter, we'll discuss the first posture.

Loosed to Love

The Posture of Repentance

Luke 7:36–50 reveals that our first posture should be one of repentance. Along with repentance comes thanksgiving for all He's done for us and all He's forgiven us for. This passage from Luke 7 is the account of the very first anointing of Jesus; it is His anointing as Prophet. Today Jesus gives us the privilege of anointing Him in the same way. When we anoint Him, our posture tells Him how we feel about Him. Let us look very carefully at this passage, because God wants us to know and understand His Word. We'll begin with verse thirty-six:

Then one of the Pharisees asked [Jesus] to eat with him. And He went to the Pharisee's house, and sat down to eat. (Luke 7:36)

First we have Jesus sitting down in Simon the Pharisee's house, at the Pharisee's invitation. Simon is a doctor of the law, and he has seen fit to invite all those who might be considered the Who's Who of his day to have lunch with him. In addition to them, he has invited Jesus. To Simon, Jesus was that Galilean who was making a name for Himself around town. I imagine that Simon wanted to check Him out to see if He was all that the people were saying about Him. So he invited Him to his house.

The custom in Palestinian days was that when someone came to your house, you treated him in a certain way. First of all, you understood that he came bearing gifts. So you didn't treat him like a nobody, because he had something you needed or wanted.

Also, when you invited someone to your house in those days, you would always greet him at the door, give him a kiss of welcome, wash his feet from the day's weary journey, anoint his head with oil to refresh him, and then allow him to sit in what amounted to an easy chair, kind of "laid back and relaxed."

On this particular day, Simon has invited all of his friends and Jesus. The table is set. Simon is enjoying the fellowship with his brethren, talking about what men talk about, talking Pharisee talk. But as they are fellowshipping with each other, over in a corner, there is Someone who is being totally ignored. He is present, and He has brought gifts with Him, but nobody is paying any attention to Him. The others are glad to see one another. To use the language of today, I can imagine them saying things like: "Man, we had a great time at the service." "I tell you, we've got some choir, haven't we?" "Didn't Pastor preach!" "Who won that game last week?" "Who do you think is going to win tomorrow?" But Jesus sits alone.

> *And behold, a woman in the city who was a sinner, when she knew that Jesus sat at the table in the Pharisee's house, brought an alabaster flask ["box,"* KJV] *of fragrant oil.* (Luke 7:37)

Then this woman of the city comes in with an alabaster box of fragrant oil that she has spent a lot of money on. The alabaster box that holds the oil represents the honor that God wants us to give Jesus—not just because He's present, but because He is worthy of our attention, our immediate attention, before anything else. We have to show Him the honor that is due Him.

And so she comes in bringing the alabaster box. In it is oil and perfume that she has saved up a whole year's salary for. Notice that she is not bringing something that did not cost her anything. The praise, the honor, that we bring to Jesus should come from a heart that says, "Lord, not only are You worthy, but I am so unworthy. And yet here is my best."

119

[She] *stood at His feet behind Him weeping; and she began to wash His feet with her tears, and wiped them with the hair of her head.* (Luke 7:38)

This woman, a sinner, comes in with a humble spirit that indicates, "I know I've messed up; I know I've done wrong; but this man is a prophet. I know enough about Him to know that He is able to forgive, and He is able to cleanse my sin. If I can just get to His feet and let Him know how much I want forgiveness, I will receive mercy. My broken heart and my contrite spirit will get His attention because He resists the proud and gives grace to the humble." She comes in thinking about what she's done wrong. She doesn't come in high and puffed up; she doesn't say, "Oh, I'm so glad I'm not like other people."

Recognizing our own sin is the first order, the first posture, of worship, because it is an attitude of gratitude, a spirit of humility. When we fall in love with the Lord, we

> Recognizing our own sin is the first posture of worship.

are willing to anoint and worship Him as a Prophet. That means we're willing to worship Him when we're broken and ashamed, even when we haven't done everything right. As we worship, we anoint Him in our broken but loving condition. A broken heart and contrite spirit He will not despise (Psalm 51:17). He expects us to humble ourselves and our hearts, and to come to Him, saying, "Lord Jesus, I know You're able to forgive sin." It's the same thing you had to do when you first came to Him for salvation.

When sinners first come to Him, they have to anoint Him as the Prophet. They get down on their knees, and they say, "I'm not worthy." They don't come happy; they don't come glad, grinning, waving, or standing as if they owned the world. They come understanding that, indeed, *"the wages of sin is death"* (Romans 6:23), and that we deserve death, but that *"the gift of God is eternal life in Christ Jesus"* (v. 23). He is the only One who was offered for us. He is the One, the only One, who can forgive us.

This woman knocked at Simon's door, came in, and did not apologize for who she was. She intruded upon everything that was going on and did not even feel bad about the fact that the men did not want her to be there. There are probably some people who don't want you to get what God has for you, either, but it really doesn't matter, because no one can stop you! It really doesn't matter what you've done or haven't done, what sins you've committed. Through true repentance, you can receive forgiveness and get rid of those sins. First, get the attitude about sin that God has. Don't try to excuse it, but call it what it is. Then, if you're willing to forsake your sins and come to God, you will be forgiven.

Even those of us who have been saved for years need God's forgiveness every day for things that we've said or thought, for our lack of faith, and for things we've done or left undone. We never outgrow our need for His grace. We have to come into a place where our hearts are broken and our spirits are dependent upon Him for forgiveness. Never outgrowing the need for forgiveness, never getting too high to be penitent—that is the posture of worship. That is the attitude He wants us to have when we bow down before Him. The Bible says that the woman washed His feet with her tears. In order to get that far down, you've got to be able to see nothing but the ground. God doesn't want us to be looking at each other, but at Him.

When we want to gain His attention, He doesn't want us to be looking at our accomplishments, either; He wants us to see our shortcomings in the light of His mercy. He wants us to be glad that we have an opportunity just to kneel before Him, and to tell Him, "Lord, I thank You.

Forgive me, because I've come short of Your glory. I want You to be refreshed by my worship. Even if nobody else wants to tell You how much he loves and appreciates You, I'm the one who's here to pour love and appreciation on You. I'm the one who's here to saturate You with love. I want Your feet to be refreshed. I realize that I'm not where I'm supposed to be. I'm not yet all that I'm called to be. I'm still growing, and I'm still faltering; I'm still making mistakes, but God, just give me another chance. Lift me up and prepare me to be what You're calling me to be."

God Word teaches us that we have to be able to give Him our highest praise; we must give God the glory that's due His name. Nothing is too good for Him. You and I have to let Him know that, no matter what it takes, this is our desire: We just want to be close to Him. We just want to be at His feet. We just want to serve Him.

We all have glory to give God. In one place, the Bible says that a woman's glory is her hair (1 Corinthians 11:15). And in this passage from Luke, we see that the woman wet Jesus' feet with her tears and dried them with her hair. She gave to Jesus out of her glory. You and I also have glory to give Him, the glory that's due His name.

Just as the woman poured out her tears on Jesus' feet, everybody ought to have a time of sorrow for sin, a time of repentance. Even when you're coming into the sanctuary, before you get to clapping and jumping and running, you should have a time where you sit and look at Him, and think about all the things in which you've come short. We need to say, "God, I need You every hour; I need You to forgive me for my transgression. *Create in me a clean heart, O God; and renew a right spirit within me*' (Psalm 51:10 KJV). God, I know I cussed somebody out the other day, and I know I got an attitude in the parking lot; I know that I was rude to the ushers; I know that I still haven't forgiven Jimmy; I know that I'm worried. But God, right now, take my mind and take my heart, and let me just focus on who You are. If You had dealt with me according to my sins, I wouldn't be here. I want to thank You, God. Lord Jesus, thank You for giving me a chance now."

When a sinner comes to Him, the angels hold their breaths, and they wait. They know that when a sinner's penitent heart is open before God, even if there are ninety-nine other people who aren't in need of repentance, even if there is a whole group of people with him who are already saved, He still waits to hear the sinner cry, "Forgive me, Lord; save me; save me!" And when the sinner cries out to Him, it's His favorite song of all; it's the song of the redeemed, because He has already shed His blood, and He is able to forgive.

> When a sinner cries out to God, it's His favorite song of all— it's the song of the redeemed.

This woman knew that Jesus was the Prophet of salvation. She anointed Him while the others were going about their business, having church as usual, fellowshipping as usual, going about life as usual.

> *She kissed His feet and anointed them with the fragrant oil. Now when the Pharisee who had invited Him saw this, he spoke to himself, saying, "This man, if He were a prophet, would know who and what manner of woman this is who is touching Him, for she is a sinner."* (Luke 7:38–39)

As you bow before the Lord and give Him your heart of repentance, as everybody ought to, you need to understand that there are some folks who are going to look at you, and they are going to say of Jesus: "Now, surely, He couldn't possibly bless her." "Surely, she shouldn't be allowed to worship." "Surely, he shouldn't be allowed to sing." "Surely, she shouldn't be shouting like that."

What do they know? Even if they know what you've done, they don't know where your heart is. Even more importantly, they don't know where Jesus' heart is toward you. While Simon is over there thinking in his heart that surely Jesus must know that this woman is a sinner, the woman is receiving something that Simon missed. Simon is way over there on the other side of the room, and he has the fellowship of his brethren, but she has the fellowship of Jesus. She has the attention of Jesus. Tell yourself, "I've got to have His attention. Even if it means I have to talk to Him about what I did wrong, I've got to have His attention. Even if it means I have to tell Him how much I love Him and appreciate Him for forgiving me for things that others don't even know I've done, I've got to have His attention. I want to know that my sins are forgiven."

Now, even while Simon is thinking in his heart that Jesus ought to know that the woman is a sinner, Jesus is waiting for an opportunity to teach as the Master Teacher. While the woman is still kneeling,

> Jesus answered and said to him, "Simon, I have something to say to you." So he said, "Teacher, say it." "There was a certain creditor who had two debtors. One owed five hundred denarii, and the other fifty. And when they had nothing with which to repay, he freely forgave them both. Tell Me, therefore, which of them will love him more?" Simon answered and said, "I suppose the one whom he forgave more." And He said to him, "You have rightly judged."
>
> (Luke 7:40–43)

Jesus has a way of talking to those who would dare to talk about us. He has a way of putting things in their minds, reminding them of things that they themselves have done or neglected to do. And He does it so easily that He can shut the enemy's mouth when we don't even know what is being thought or said about us. In the above Scripture passage, Jesus did this merely by telling Simon a simple story: There was a man who had two debtors; two people owed him money. One owed him a little bit, and one owed him a lot, but neither one

How much you love God often depends on how much you've been forgiven for—or how much you realize you've been forgiven for.

of them could pay. And none of us can pay for what we've done. There are some people who have not sinned as much as others, but *"all have sinned and fall short of the glory of God"* (Romans 3:23). Everybody has done something wrong. Everybody owes a debt to God that he can't pay. And, quite frankly, since we cannot pay, we are all at the mercy of the true and living God. Jesus said to Simon, "The debtors couldn't pay, but do you know what? The man forgave both of them. Now, who do you think is going to love him the most?"

Even though the woman had come to Jesus for forgiveness, Simon was critical of her in his heart. However, when a sinner comes penitently before God, He closes the mouth of his adversary.

> *Then He turned to the woman and said to Simon, "Do you see this woman? I entered your house; you gave Me no water for My feet, but she has washed My feet with her tears and wiped them with the hair of her head. You gave Me no kiss, but this woman has not ceased to kiss My feet since the time I came in. You did not anoint My head with oil, but this woman has anointed My feet with fragrant oil. Therefore I say to you, her sins, which are many, are forgiven, for she loved much. But to whom little is forgiven, the same loves little." Then He said to her, "Your sins are forgiven."* (Luke 7:44–48)

How much you love God often depends on how much you've been forgiven for—or how much you *realize* you've been forgiven for. There are some Goody Two-shoes who can say, "I never drank, I never smoked, and I never ran with women; I grew up in the church; I was always a Sunday school student," and on and on. Even though they also have come short of the glory of God, they sit smugly with their hands and feet crossed, because they really don't remember their sinfulness. But those who have come through hell and high water; those who have messed up over and over again; those who could talk about their sins, but don't want to talk about them because they would have to censor what they say—God says that they love much because they have been forgiven much.

Now, this doesn't mean that you should go out and commit more sin so that you can love more. But it's often true that the more God has forgiven you for, the more you think about what He has done, and you realize that, if it hadn't been for His intervention, you would have been gone. You realize that He should have cut you off, that you don't deserve anything at all, and therefore you love Him more.

Are you someone who has many things to love God for? Are there many things that He has forgiven you for? God has forgiven me for many things, and every time I think about His forgiveness, I thank Him.

You need to know what God does for you when you anoint Him in a posture of repentance. He takes you and gives you *"beauty for ashes"* (Isaiah 61:3). He takes off the sin. He takes away the guilt. He takes away the stain. While you are anointing Him, somebody else may be looking at you funny. But while you are thanking Him for His forgiveness, while you are thanking Him for His blood, and while you are asking Him to cleanse you, He's literally washing you and taking away all the stains, taking away all the guilt. And so, even if somebody else is looking at you funny, you start to feel lighter; the burden is rolling away. As He takes the burden off you, He gives you *"beauty for ashes, the oil of joy for mourning, the garment of praise for the spirit of heaviness"* (v. 3). He puts on you the coat of many colors. He covers you with His blood and righteousness.

Therefore, even though people may start out looking at you as if you are strange, something happens as you are worshiping Him, as you are asking Him for forgiveness. They see that the more you worship, the better you look. God is able to *"beautify the humble with salvation"* (Psalm 149:4). I don't care if you messed up last night; you need to get on your face and tell Him, "God, forgive me. Lord, I love You; You're worthy. I just want to bless You. If nobody else wants to bless You, here I am; I'm willing to give You the glory." Never mind what others say; never mind what others are doing. As we worship Him, He has a way of removing the burden, and we feel lighter.

Everybody messes up, but that isn't an excuse to run from Him. He has made a way for us to be forgiven. You can come to Him and be cleansed. Worship through it, worship out from under it, worship over the top of it, and God will cleanse you. He will forgive; He is the only One who can forgive your sins. And when He forgives you, it doesn't matter what anybody else thinks. He begins to lift you up; He begins to restore your joy. Others thought you were down for the count, but now you're up and beginning to walk around, and you feel the presence of the Lord. You have been repentant before the

Everybody messes up, but that isn't an excuse to run from God.

Lord; you have lain before Him, and now the Lord has lifted up your head and given you a glorious victory. When your friends try to draw you back into the world, you can say to them, "I'm sorry, but I can't go back with you. I just came out of a session with my Savior, and He has told me that my sins are forgiven. I know they were many, but I'm so glad to tell you that I'm free."

Worship will free you. The enemy cannot bring an accusation against those who are covered by the blood. As you worship, He lifts you up. He's your glory and the lifter of your head (Psalm 3:3). *"He shall cover you with His feathers, and under His wings you shall take refuge"* (Psalm 91:4). Keep on worshiping Him. When You worship Him, He will clothe you with such splendid adornment that, even though you kneel down in ashes, you will get up in glorious victory. Then you will go from the penitent state of asking for forgiveness and giving Him thanks to the precious state of standing ready for service. You will tell Him, "Here I am, Lord. You've been a Friend to me, and I'm a friend to You. I'm ready to serve You." It's time for...

...Breaking the Alabaster Box

Chapter Eight
Breaking the Alabaster Box

In this chapter, we're going to look at the second and third postures that we need in order to experience God in His fullness: service permeated with worship, and a life committed to His Lordship. These postures correspond to our anointing Jesus not only as Prophet, but also as Priest and King. When we anoint Jesus as Priest in our lives, we recognize His goodness, and we serve others through Him as we offer Him *continual* praise. When we anoint Him as King, we honor Him as Lord; we worship Him not because of anything specific that He's done, but because He is altogether worthy of our praise.

The Posture of Worshipful Service

The first posture was repentance, but as we develop our day-to-day relationship with Him, we're not to be always crying on the altar asking for forgiveness. At this point in our spiritual maturity, there should be some things that we've overcome. He's forgiven us, and we're not going back, hallelujah! We may have something new to ask for forgiveness for next week, but it won't be the same thing. As He raises us up, and He finds that we're willing to walk in obedience, we are able to give Him the priestly anointing as we stand beside Him in service. John 12:1–7 will help us to understand more about the ministry of the priestly anointing:

> *Then, six days before the Passover, Jesus came to Bethany, where Lazarus was who had been dead, whom He had raised from the dead. There they made Him a supper; and Martha served, but Lazarus was one of those who sat at the table with Him.*
> (John 12:1–2)

In this passage, Jesus comes to Bethany, and here we find Lazarus at the table with Him. Lazarus was dead, but now he is alive, because Jesus raised him. Many other people have come to see Lazarus. (See verse 9.) They have been talking about his resurrection, and they've been trying to find out how it happened. Lazarus doesn't have anything to say. He doesn't have to, because he's a living witness.

Let me note here that there are times when you don't have to say anything; you just walk out your faith; you just live it out. There are times when you don't have to put a cross around your neck or a Bible under your arm. All you have to do is just live right, walk right, talk right, and let people see the glory of the Lord upon you. Picture the people in Bethany saying, "Look at him; look at him! Lazarus looks as if the glory of the Lord is upon him!" They are just so happy to see Lazarus, to see a miracle.

However, in the midst of the miracle that they see in Lazarus, they've forgotten about Jesus. Jesus has come, but they are looking at Lazarus. Doesn't that sound familiar? Don't you often hear people say, "Oh, did you see that woman get up and walk away from that walker?" and "Did you hear his testimony? That man was healed of cancer"? These things are good in themselves, because we're to expect signs and wonders to occur. *"These signs will follow those who believe"* (Mark 16:17), Jesus said. Demons will come out in His name. Healings will take place in His name. But these things are never to take precedence over the worship that we are to give Him, because, otherwise, you end up with people who are miracle worshipers. They follow those who are able to cast out demons. They follow those who are able to lay hands on the sick and restore them. They follow those who are able to give them a prophetic word. But the Giver is the One whom we need to go after, not the gift. He expects us not to worship the one who is able to lay hands on us for healing, because that person is not the One who really healed us. God says that we're to worship Him above all others.

We need to worship the Giver, not the gift.

Now, as the people are busy talking about Lazarus, all he does is just sit there. In the same way, people will examine you. They'll check you out. They'll try to find any kind of flaw in you that they can. They'll be looking for any inconsistency. You should respond by just living out your faith. Don't worry if they start rumors about you; don't even worry if they start telling lies about you. The truth will outlive a lie every time. Just keep on living uprightly; just keep on walking uprightly.

As the people are busy examining Lazarus,

> *they made* [Jesus] *a supper; and Martha served.*
> (John 12:2)

You have to have the heart of a servant. And if you really want to have the heart of a servant, you have to understand what being a servant is all about. A servant is not one who is lazy, but one who comes and says, "May I help you?" "Please, may I get you some water?" "May I visit you?" "May I come take care of your children?" And in the passage from John, *"Martha served."* She's busy serving. She's taking good care of the gentlemen gathered there.

However, there's more to servanthood than keeping busy or even helping others. Martha was the one who was *"distracted with much serving"* (Luke 10:40). There are some people who are so preoccupied with doing and doing and doing for the Lord that they never worship Him. They love to lead in prayer, but they never really pray. They love to lead worship, but they are never really worshiping as they lead. God wants us to understand that the doing and the serving are good, but they can never take the place of our worship, and of our ministry of anointing. Worship and service have to go together.

> *Then Mary took a pound of very costly oil of spike-nard, anointed the feet of Jesus, and wiped His feet with her hair.* (John 12:3)

Even in the midst of the busy work of ministry, there are those whose attitude is, "I'm going to wipe His feet. I'm going to make sure that Jesus gets all the attention that He needs." Even in the midst of a church service, even in the midst of ministry, even in the midst of going to the prisons, even in the midst of visiting people in the hospital, even in the midst of bringing in the homeless, even in the midst of driving the church bus or directing traffic in the parking lot, these servants of God feel they need to anoint His feet. They feel they need to give Him some attention. They feel they must make sure He knows that, even though they're serving, even though they're working in the house of the Lord, they need to worship Him. There is something about someone who is constantly giving the Lord praise and giving the Lord worship, even while he or she is working.

These servants of God are living on a higher level of communion with Him. You see, there are some folks who will come into the house of the Lord, and they will worship while the music is playing, but when they are in the parking lot directing traffic, it's an entirely different thing. You have to have an attitude that says to God, "You're worthy all the time: You're worthy while I'm working. You're worthy while I'm walking. You're worthy while I'm lifting groceries into my car. You're worthy while I'm cleaning the trash cans. You're worthy, O God."

> *And the house was filled with the fragrance of the oil.* (John 12:3)

Mary anointed Jesus' feet with the costly oil, and the fragrance of the oil filled the room. The fragrance was so sweet that everyone in the room could experience her worship.

When was the last time your worship made somebody else happy? You don't really intend for it to make others happy, because you're not concerned about whether they are listening to you or not; you are lifting your praise to God alone. But when your worship becomes so good that it starts to overflow and fill the room, and you are giving Jesus much love and attention, those sitting next to you will catch a glimpse of His glory on you, and they will start getting happy.

Have you ever sat next to somebody who was worshiping the Lord in this way, so much so that it was contagious? You could almost smell it; you could almost feel it. You sensed the excitement; you knew that something was happening. Even if it wasn't happening for you, there was something inside you that made you want it to happen for you. And you started thinking, "If I could just get a taste of what that person is experiencing, then I'd feel like I'm going to be all right."

God is saying to us, "I want you to understand that when you really worship as you're walking, as you're working, as you're taking care of the children, as you're signing for the deaf ministry, or whatever else you might be doing, everybody around you is going to begin to want what you have. Everybody around you is going to start looking at you, and they are going to see how transparent you are."

You will not be a closet Christian, and you will not be somebody who worships just on Sundays. You will say, "I'm wide open. I worship everywhere; I worship anywhere; I will give the Lord glory because He's worthy." Then others will smell the fragrant oil of your worship. You'll make them feel as if they're missing something as they watch you bless the Lord. You will make them jealous, so that they'll begin to do what you're doing. If you're willing to do that, I promise you that the fragrance of your worship will change the atmosphere where you are.

The fragrance of your worship will change the atmosphere around you.

You can begin to anoint the Lord at any time by blessing Him. Tell Him, "God, I'm with You. God, I thank You for being my Friend. I'm here to serve You. Lord, whatever You want me to do, I'm ready; I'm willing. And Father, while I'm doing it, I just want You to know that I'm going to let a sweet-smelling fragrance come out of my lips. I'm going to let everybody know that I'm worshiping You. I don't mind if they know it; I want them to know it. I want them to be blessed by my worship. I want You to be blessed. And I want others to join me in anointing You."

If many are anointing the Lord with their worship, we don't have to depend on two or three people to carry the load. Everybody in the house of the Lord ought to bring about a change in the atmosphere; everybody should be anointing the Lord, giving God drippings of oil.

Give God some perfume to let Him know that you're present in His house. Say to Him, "Even if nobody else wants to worship, I brought my oil; it cost me something, but You're worthy. Others can laugh at me while I'm worshiping, but I don't care, because You're worthy. You've been my Friend. I want to let the world know that I am not ashamed of You."

I know you're not ashamed to worship. I know you're not ashamed to cry. I know you're not ashamed to bless Him. I know you'll bless Him in church, and I know you'll bless Him at your job, because you are a worshiper, and worshipers don't know the difference between Sunday and Tuesday. Worshipers can't tell the difference between day and night. Every day is Sunday to a worshiper.

> *And the house was filled with the fragrance of the oil.* (John 12:3)

Let the house be filled. Can you smell His presence? Let the house be filled with the fragrance. Let Him know that you love Him. Let Him know that you need Him. Let Him know that you honor Him. He is the aroma that we live for. His presence is what we seek. And when we fill the house of the Lord with praise, He comes. He comes bringing healing, not just for you, but also for the person standing next to you.

We must understand that we are not worshiping just for ourselves. We are worshiping so that the whole house might be filled with His glory. We are worshiping for the sinner standing next to us, so that he will become jealous of our relationship with the Lord and want to know Him, too. We are worshiping for the sick ones standing beside us, so that they will be healed.

Let the weak say, "I am strong in the presence of the Lord." (See Joel 3:10.) Our exposed worship, our transparent worship, frees God to bless those who are beside us. We can't be ashamed of worshiping Him, because it leads us to the final level of anointing, where we anoint Him as the King. However, understand that there are some who will be indignant at your transparent worship. They'll think you're showing off. They won't know, they won't care, about the reality of your worship. They'll be like Judas, thinking that you shouldn't have spent so much, that you shouldn't go that far in your worship. (See John 12:4–6.) But we really can't go far enough. We need to show Him the honor that He truly deserves.

My little body can't give enough praise. My little mouth just can't bless Him enough. My hands can't wave enough. My knees can't bow enough, but I'm going to do the best I can. And if our praise bothers someone else, that's all right, because He promises us He'll tell people: "Leave him alone. You don't know, like he knows, what I've done for him"; "Leave her alone. You weren't there when I communed with her"; "You don't have any idea why he is crying so hard; leave him alone. It's not because he's done anything wrong; it's because I've done everything right. Leave him alone." *"Let her alone. Why do you trouble her? She has done a good work for Me....She has done what she could"* (Mark 14:6, 8; see also John 12:7–8).

Go ahead and worship; let the tears flow. Nobody knows what you've been through, and nobody has to know. When you cry, maybe it will free others to cry. When you wave, maybe it will free others to lift their hands to God. When you open your mouth, maybe it will free others to go ahead and let what's inside them come out.

The Posture of Honoring His Lordship

Anointing Him as Priest will bring us to a place where we're able to anoint Him as King of our lives. When we arrive at this place, we're not just willing to serve Him, but we're also willing to commit our lives to His Lordship; we anoint Him not because of anything He's done, but because He is altogether worthy of our praise.

In the fourteenth chapter of Mark, there is yet another account of a woman who anoints Jesus:

> *And being in Bethany at the house of Simon the leper, as He sat at the table, a woman came having an alabaster flask ["box," KJV] of very costly oil of spikenard. Then she broke the flask and poured it on His head. But there were some who were indignant among themselves, and said, "Why was this fragrant oil wasted? For it might have been sold for more than three hundred denarii and given to the poor." And they criticized her sharply. But Jesus said, "Let her alone. Why do you trouble her? She has done a good work for Me. For you have the poor with you always, and whenever you wish you may do them good; but Me you do not have always. She has done what she could. She has come beforehand to anoint My body for burial. Assuredly, I say to you, wherever this gospel is preached in the whole world, what this woman has done will also be told as a memorial to her."*
>
> (Mark 14:3–9)

This woman comes to the house of Simon the leper in Bethany, where Jesus is having a meal, and everybody watches as she breaks her alabaster box and pours oil on Jesus' head. The time has come when a little oil is not going to be enough. The Bible says that the woman took the box and broke it. That means that she was not holding anything back anymore. Although her action foretold Jesus' coming crucifixion and served to anoint His body for burial, her heart was also anointing Him as King because she recognized that He was altogether worthy of her love and honor. She held nothing back in her worship of Him.

There comes a time when you have to break your alabaster box and let it all go—you and your little conservative self, you and your little sophisticated, aristocratic self. You are going to have to break it up and let it go. You are going to have to open up everything you've been holding in. God has been too good for you to hold back now.

I can hear Jesus saying, "I deserve to hear your worship. I deserve to have it. You're not coming just to anoint My feet now; you're not coming just to anoint Me because I pray for you. You're coming to anoint Me even if I don't do anything else for you. You're coming to anoint Me as the King of Kings because you know I'm worthy. You know there is nobody like Me. You know that I'm over you. You know that I'm the One you adore. I'm the One you live for. I'm the One you're committing your life to. I'm the One you will obey no matter what. If I say 'Run,' you'll run. If I say, 'Leap,' you'll leap. If I say, 'Follow your faith,' you're going to follow your faith, because you're willing to crown me as King of your life.

> God has been too good for you to hold back now.

"You know that when you're willing to rely on Me and worship Me as King, you're making a lifestyle commitment. You're making a commitment not just as a praiser, but also as a worshiper. You're making a commitment to worship Me not just on Sunday, but every day. Worshipers walk right. Worshipers witness every chance they get. Worshipers are not ashamed. Worshipers stand in the gate; they stand in the gap. Worshipers pray for those who oppose them. Worshipers entrust themselves to God so completely that they're not merely involved, they're moving past involvement and on to commitment."

There's the story about a man who ordered ham and eggs. The man was very hungry, and he was so glad when his order arrived that he told the waiter, "I'm so thankful for this plate of ham and eggs." The waiter said to him, "Yeah, but you need to know something. The chicken who laid the eggs so that you could eat got involved, but the pig was totally committed to your breakfast. He gave his life." You can be involved, and you can even lay a few eggs, but when you're committed, you lay down your life.

We need to say to the Lord, "You've given me life. Therefore, I am no longer just going to be involved. King of my life, I crown You now. I want my life—not just my deeds, not just my words, not just my praise—I want my life to crown You King every day. I want my life itself to be praise to You." The time has come when God is not only looking for praisers and worshipers (and He is looking for them), but He is also looking for those who will let their lives be praise, who will let their lives be a worshipful offering to Him. (See Isaiah 43:19–21; 62:6–7.)

When this happens, you realize that you're praising Him all the time; you're worshiping Him all the time. In the good times and in the bad times; when you're good, and when you're not so good; when you feel as if you've been on top of the world, and when you feel as if the world has been on top of you; you are still worshiping Him. Something new has happened. Now you're *living* a lifestyle of praise and worship. In other words, you are carrying Him around everywhere, talking to Him and talking about Him. Your very life has become praise!

At this point, God knows He can trust you to worship Him anywhere through a lifestyle of praise. This means that you watch what you do, you watch where you walk, and you watch how you walk. Even while you are working on your job, you can't help but give Him worthy praise. You don't let yourself do the things that you used to do. You say, "I know God, I love Him, and I've got to

141

give Him the glory that's due His name. I'm going to worship my Savior."

Worship becomes your life. Everywhere you go, you expect to give Him glory. You'll say, "If you wake me up at three o'clock in the morning, I have a sacrifice of praise to offer. If you see me at five o'clock in the afternoon, in the middle of rush hour, I still have an offering of praise, because He's building a lifestyle of worship in me." You have to kill the flesh to do that, so that you can look at somebody who has just made you really angry, and say, "That's all right. I will praise the Lord; I will worship the Lord."

Having a lifestyle of praise means that you will give Him a continual offering of worship, as the priests did in the tabernacle of David. (See 1 Chronicles 16:4–6.) That doesn't mean you'll necessarily walk around saying "Praise the Lord!" "Hallelujah!" "Thank You, Jesus!" and "Glory!" all the time; but worship will always be in your mouth; it will always be there. It's like a spout. All you have to do is open your mouth and it comes out.

God will be able to count on continual praise from you. You have become His ark of the covenant in the earth. You are bearing His presence. His presence in you has begun to overflow. When people see you coming, they see that you've been in His presence, that you are carrying His glory. When you have your hands lifted up to praise Him, His glory rests on your shoulders, as it rested with the ark of the covenant between the cherubim that leaned over the top of the mercy seat. Let me repeat what I said: *the glory of God will rest upon you.*

Let that thought sink in for a moment. Then I want you to recall the fact that He first waits for you to anoint Him as Prophet. Be careful not to be self-righteous. Tell Him how much you appreciate His shed blood and the cleansing power of His Word. Then, anoint Him as Priest.

Stand beside Him, serve, and become involved in the lives and needs of others. That is your worship: *"Present your bodies a living sacrifice, holy, acceptable to God, which is your reasonable service"* (Romans 12:1). The Greek word for *"service"* indicates worship.

When you worship, *"do not be conformed to this world, but be transformed by the renewing of your mind"* (v. 2). That means, don't be what people expect you to be. Don't let them squeeze you into their mold. People may say that you shouldn't praise, that worship is not appropriate, but it's always appropriate. If they say, "It's against our policies," forget the policies; it's better to obey God than to obey man (Acts 5:29). And God says that when we please Him, He will make even our enemies to be at peace with us (Proverbs 16:7). I promise you, worshipers always win. He'll break open a prison for a worshiper. He'll shut the mouth of a lion for a worshiper. Worship Him in spirit and in truth, and crown Him King of your life.

> Worshipers always win, so worship Him in spirit and in truth.

God is looking for someone who wants his or her life to be a praise to Him. I challenge you to break your alabaster box and begin to anoint the Lord. Anoint Him as the Prophet of your life. Anoint Him as your High Priest. Anoint Him as your King. He's waiting for you. I urge you to let Him hear your praise and feel your love. If you want your whole life to be a praise to God, then just tell Him so. Present yourself to Him; open your mouth and anoint Him with your worship. Let Him know you are in His house. Tell Him, "Here I am, Lord. Thank You for forgiveness. Thank You for the *'new and living way'* (Hebrews 10:20). Thank You that You are not only able to consecrate me, but that You are also able to take me to a deeper place in You. Thank You, Lord."

Break that box; let Him in. Go through the gate; press your way. Love Him just for who He is. He is listening for your praise and worship. Start right now.

Every day, you owe Him some time just to make love to Him. Find a song, find some words, find something from your spirit to let Him know that He is the King of your life, that He is the forgiving One, that He is the Priest that you depend upon. Let Him know how much you love Him. And while you're doing that, I promise you, you won't be able to bring any reproach on His name. You'll be able to walk even more closely to Him. You'll be able to see Him even more clearly than before. And, as you worship with others, you will experience...

...Glory in Unity

Chapter Nine

Glory in Unity

We are the worshipers who have dared to enter into His gates! *"Enter into His gates with thanksgiving, and into His courts with praise. Be thankful to Him, and bless His name"* (Psalm 100:4). We have anointed Him as our Prophet, Priest, and King.

The Perfection of Worship

We have progressed from the *pattern* to the *posture* of worship, and now we are to go on to the *perfection* of worship. This perfection is manifested as we become living praise, and as we show forth God's glory through our worship in unity with other believers.

Reflecting His Glory

We have to bring worship to its completion and fulfillment. It's an everyday process. We have to understand that God is working on us twenty-four hours a day, seven days a week, because He is taking us from the tabernacle of Moses to the temple of Solomon, which represents the place where His glory is seen.

Solomon's temple was twice as big as the tabernacle of Moses. Similarly, God wants us to spiritually stretch

147

ourselves and expand. He is perfecting that which pertains to our giving Him glory. He doesn't want us just to give Him praise; He's working on us so that we will *become* praise. He is going to turn us into a reflection of His glory (2 Corinthians 3:18). When people see us coming, we won't even have to say, "Hallelujah!"; they'll look at us, and *they'll* say, "Hallelujah!"

The Spirit of Solomon

The process of the building of the temple reveals much about how we are to go on to perfection in worship. In 1 Chronicles 29:13–23, David, who was about to turn the kingdom over to his son, Solomon, prayed to God concerning the preparations for the building of the temple, after the people had willingly donated materials for it.

> *"Now therefore, our God, we thank You and praise Your glorious name. But who am I, and who are my people, that we should be able to offer so willingly as this? For all things come from You, and of Your own we have given You. For we are aliens and pilgrims before You, as were all our fathers; our days on earth are as a shadow, and without hope. O LORD our God, all this abundance that we have prepared to build You a house for Your holy name is from Your hand, and is all Your own. I know also, my God, that You test the heart and have pleasure in uprightness. As for me, in the uprightness of my heart I have willingly offered all these things; and now with joy I have seen Your people, who are present here to offer willingly to You. O LORD God of Abraham, Isaac, and Israel, our fathers, keep this forever in the intent of the thoughts of the heart of Your people, and fix their heart toward You. And give my son Solomon a loyal heart to keep Your commandments and Your testimonies and Your*

statutes, to do all these things, and to build the temple for which I have made provision." Then David said to all the assembly, "Now bless the LORD your God." So all the assembly blessed the LORD God of their fathers, and bowed their heads and prostrated themselves before the LORD and the king. And they made sacrifices to the LORD and offered burnt offerings to the LORD on the next day: a thousand bulls, a thousand rams, a thousand lambs, with their drink offerings, and sacrifices in abundance for all Israel. So they ate and drank before the LORD with great gladness on that day. And they made Solomon the son of David king the second time, and anointed him before the LORD to be the leader, and Zadok to be priest. Then Solomon sat on the throne of the LORD as king instead of David his father, and prospered; and all Israel obeyed him.

First, God wants us to see that He has established us with the same mindset that David had to praise and worship the Lord. But as much as David loved God, he was not allowed to build the temple, because he had been a man of war, a man who had shed blood. (See 1 Chronicles 28:2–3.) He was also a man who had had trouble with the flesh. David's son, Solomon, was chosen by God to build the temple instead. Why? Because Solomon's spirit was different. He had the spirit of a tender plant, an innocent one. He was not a person who sought glory. When God told Solomon He would grant whatever request he would ask for, instead of asking for riches, instead of asking for fame and fortune, instead of asking for the heads of his enemies, he asked for wisdom, the principal thing, because he knew that if he could just get God's wisdom, he could handle the holy things. The holy things represent the people God gives to our care. (See 1 Kings 3:3–14.)

> People are holy things, and you have to handle them with wisdom.

People are holy things, and you have to handle them with wisdom. You have to be able to handle them with tenderness; you have to handle them as God would handle them. Our perspective should be that God is the only God, that He is the only Judge, and that therefore He expects us to treat each other as He would treat us. He expects us to be tender with each other.

David, however, had usurped Uriah. He had taken advantage of him, committed adultery with his wife, and then had him killed. David had also killed many in battle. David was not the one who was qualified to build the temple, but Solomon was. And it is those who have the humble, gentle spirit of Solomon's early days who are given the opportunity by God to move to the next level of worship.

No Flesh Can Glory in God's Presence

You can't go to the next level with bloody hands. You're going to have to wash your hands. You're going to have to wash your hearts. You're going to have to let God purge you and get rid of the evil motives, the vindictiveness, the malice, the unforgiveness, anything that the flesh would dare to hold on to. I hear God saying, "Where I'm taking you, no flesh can glory in My presence. You are going to have to leave your flesh outside the door."

Now, when David realized that he could not build the temple, he did not get upset, because he understood the holiness of God. He collected all of the materials necessary to build the temple, even though he understood he wasn't going to build it, and he still had enough praise and glory and honor for the Lord to understand that God's way must be fulfilled. We need to have the same attitude. When you realize that you're not yet in the place that God has called you to be, but you see that somebody else is, God will say to you, "Please don't get an attitude, because if you're willing to lie before Me in humility, I will give you a new heart. I'll create in you a new spirit. I'll give you a tender heart. You're proud and puffed up right now; you're always vengeful; you always have to have your way, but you don't have to stay in that condition. Just come to Me, and watch Me turn things around for you." He will give us the spirit of Solomon so that we can go on to the next level of worship.

God is not satisfied with our jumping around and praising and worshiping Him, and then treating each other without love and tenderness, treating each other as if we're not deserving of what God has given us. God wants us to give others the same grace that He has given us. He wants us to show others the same mercy that He has showed us. He wants us to extend to others the same forgiveness He has extended to us. In fact, He says, "I won't even forgive you if you won't forgive your brother or sister. I want you to treat them as I have treated you." (See Matthew 6:15.)

> God wants us to give others the same grace that He has given us.

Just as an exchange of kings took place and Solomon became ruler of Israel in place of David, an exchange of what rules our hearts and lives has to take place. Our flesh has to die in order for this exchange to take place, so that we can move on to glory. We need to have the spirit of Solomon. We have to move on to perfection. Beloved, we can't keep running around the same old track, taking the same old lap, doing the same old things, over and over again. It's time now to move on, just as David passed the mantle on to Solomon.

God is working in our lives to bring us to the next level. He's establishing the spirit of Solomon in each and every one of us, and that spirit understands that we are not our own. We belong to God, and everything we have comes from Him. As David said,

> *All things come from You, and of Your own we have given You.*　　　　　　　　(1 Chronicles 29:14)

Our attitude toward God is to be, "It's not my money; it's not my talent; it came from You, and so I willingly offer it back to You. Nobody has to twist my arm; nobody has to make me give what You have given to me; I give it with a loving heart." With that perspective, nothing is impossible to people who believe their God, know their God, and worship their God. They *"shall be strong, and do exploits"* (Daniel 11:32 KJV).

Glory and Unity

In this hour when God calls us to the temple of Solomon, we need to realize that the concept of glory is tied to unity. This is a time for gathering believers together and helping them understand that we need all of them if we're truly to move on to the next level. It's not just a matter of you doing your thing and me doing my thing. Everything that's going to happen in the temple of Solomon has an "all" clause attached to it.

When Solomon became king, *all* of the people worshiped God, and they bowed down before both God and the king. This is significant, because they showed worth-ship to God first; they worshiped Him with the glory that was due His name, and then they turned right around and honored the king, who was Solomon, and let him know that they cared just as much for him as he was to care for them. It was as if they were saying, "We don't minimize you at all. As a matter of fact, we are going to

152

worship God and bring everything that we have for the building of the temple. Then God is going to bless us and enable us to give you whatever your heart desires, whatever the vision God has given you calls for. After we've worshiped our God, we'll be able to build this temple, take the land, and do whatever you have in your mind, mighty leader."

Beloved, it's going to take all of us. You have to be a part of the "all." All of us have to bow down; all of us have to give God glory, and all of us should honor our spiritual leaders.

David turned the kingdom over to Solomon, and the plans for the temple were completed. The people had their priorities straight. They didn't worship the king as a celebrity; they gave him the honor that was due him, and they worshiped the Lord God with the glory that was due Him.

> The leaders of the fathers' houses, leaders of the tribes of Israel, the captains of thousands and of hundreds, with the officers over the king's work, offered willingly. They gave for the work of the house of God five thousand talents and ten thousand darics of gold, ten thousand talents of silver, eighteen thousand talents of bronze, and one hundred thousand talents of iron. And whoever had precious stones gave them to the treasury of the house of the LORD, into the hand of Jehiel the Gershonite. Then the people rejoiced, for they had offered willingly, because with a loyal heart they had offered willingly to the Lord....And they made sacrifices to the LORD and offered burnt offerings to the LORD on the next day: a thousand bulls, a thousand rams, a thousand lambs, with their drink offerings, and sacrifices in abundance for all Israel. So they ate and drank before the LORD with great gladness on that day. And they made Solomon the son of David king the second time, and anointed him before the LORD

to be the leader, and Zadok to be priest. Then Solo-
mon sat on the throne of the LORD as king instead
of David his father, and prospered; and all Israel
obeyed him. All the leaders and the mighty men,
and also all the sons of King David, submitted
themselves to King Solomon.
(1 Chronicles 29:6–9, 21–24)

All of Israel gave willingly to the Lord for the building of the temple. They ate and drank and were merry, but the bottom line was that they obeyed the man of God. You can eat, you can drink, and you'll be merry, but you're going to miss out if you don't obey.

Stop Counting

The Word says that Israel sacrificed to the Lord. They sacrificed so much that they stopped counting; there were *"sacrifices in abundance for all Israel"* (1 Chronicles 29:21).

We are not to count what we give God. We say, "Well, you know, I gave twenty-five dollars. And I handed someone a brick when they were constructing the building. I mean, you did see me hand someone a brick, didn't you?" But we should stop counting, because we are at the point now where we ought to give just because we have it to give and because we want God's kingdom to advance. We don't count; we're not concerned about it. We keep on giving until it gets done. We don't compare ourselves to Mary Lou and tell her, "I gave ten dollars, and you haven't even given five dollars." No, at the next level of worship, we're going to give and give and give. If God keeps on giving to us, we're going to keep on giving it back to His work. We're going to keep on pouring it back, because you can't outgive God no matter how you try. Don't compare yourself with anybody else, and don't

154

count anymore. Stop counting, and God will give you so much that you won't be able to count it.

There are some things MasterCard can buy. There are some things you can get with Visa or American Express. But what God is getting ready to give us is priceless; you can't pay for it. When you stop counting and just keep on giving whatever God tells you to give, He will bring you into the Holy of Holies and let you touch the manifested presence of who He is. When God puts true worship into you, and you start experiencing Him like you never have before, money won't mean anything to you. Difficult people won't mean anything to you. Inconvenience won't mean anything to you. Getting a parking space at church won't mean anything to you; you'll be glad just to be in the worship service. You'll press your way past everything in order to be in His presence, and to give Him all He asks for!

When God puts true worship in us, nothing will prevent us from coming into His presence.

You'll spend so much time worshiping Him during the week, that when the church doors open on Sunday and you come through the door—I don't mean when you get to your seat, but when you come through the door, or even before you hit the door, when you're in the parking lot—you will be entering His gates with thanksgiving, and coming into His courts with praise. By the time you get to your seat, your seat won't hold you, because you will be thanking Him so and blessing His name. You will be glad, holy, and happy to show His worth-ship.

The Revealed Glory of God

Now, because Israel gave willingly, honored God and the king, and were obedient, God allowed them to finish the work of the temple in short order.

So all the work that Solomon had done for the house of the LORD was finished; and Solomon brought in the things which his father David had dedicated: the silver and the gold and all the furnishings. And he put them in the treasuries of the house of God. Now Solomon assembled the elders of Israel and all the heads of the tribes, the chief fathers of the children of Israel, in Jerusalem, that they might bring the ark of the covenant of the LORD up from the City of David, which is Zion. Therefore all the men of Israel assembled with the king at the feast, which was in the seventh month. So all the elders of Israel came, and the Levites took up the ark. Then they brought up the ark, the tabernacle of meeting, and all the holy furnishings that were in the tabernacle. The priests and the Levites brought them up.

(2 Chronicles 5:1–5)

"So all the work that Solomon had done for the house of the LORD was finished" (v. 1). When they finished the work, they brought the ark of the covenant to the temple from the City of David. They brought the presence of the Lord into the temple. God is working on us so that He can have us ready for the day of dedication. D-day is coming. And when it comes, you can't have the same attitudes you had before. God is going to have to be able to count on us to obey the Word. Be a doer of the Word, so that, when the temple is finished, when the presence of the Lord that is in us manifests itself, the glory of God will be revealed.

Let's skip down now to verse eleven: *"And it came to pass when the priests came out of the Most Holy Place (for all the priests who were present had sanctified themselves, without keeping to their divisions)."* These priests didn't wait for the usher to usher them down. They didn't wait for the offering to be taken. They didn't wait for the altar call, either. They sanctified themselves.

The Levites who were the singers, all those of Asaph and Heman and Jeduthun, with their sons and their brethren, stood at the east end of the altar, clothed in white linen, having cymbals, stringed instruments and harps, and with them one hundred and twenty priests sounding with trumpets; indeed it came to pass, when the trumpeters and singers were as one, to make one sound to be heard in praising and thanking the LORD, and when they lifted up their voice with the trumpets and cymbals and instruments of music, and praised the LORD, saying: "For He is good, for His mercy endures forever," that the house, the house of the LORD, was filled with a cloud, so that the priests could not continue ministering because of the cloud; for the glory of the LORD filled the house of God. (2 Chronicles 5:12–14)

Note that the text says, *"The trumpeters and singers were as one, to make one sound to be heard in praising and thanking the LORD."* In other words, when we start praising Him together, and thanking Him together, with all of the instruments, and we say, "[The Lord] *is good, for His mercy endures forever"* (v. 13), then the glory of the Lord will fill the house— God will fill us with His glory. The people didn't have to wait for somebody to lay hands on them for them to experience God's glory, because the presence of the Lord was being embraced. We are His people. We are His priests. He has called us together to make one sound. Unity is the last garment God is going to put on us before He reveals His glory.

> Unity is the last garment God is going to put on us before He reveals His glory.

When we celebrate our God, we use everything that we can think of to *"make His praise glorious"* (Psalm 66:2), such as songs, instruments, and dance. All the believers gathered together are to participate together in this worship. God wants us to have the kind of experience where everyone participates, so that we will be able to worship with all of the kindred and tongues and tribes that we are getting ready to be united with in the twinkling of an eye, when we all get to heaven.

What a time that will be. We won't worry about the color of anyone's skin; we'll just be blessing and praising, and whatever kind of worship is going on at a given moment, we'll be involved in it. We'll be able to dance with our messianic Jewish brothers and sisters. We'll be able to worship with all our brothers and sisters of every denomination. In fact, I believe that, even before this is a reality in heaven, all the churches of God will come together in a final revival that God is sending to this earth, which is a revival of worship.

Unity Brings the Anointing

We must join together in unified corporate worship. A spirit of unity needs to overtake those who gather for worship, because a corporate spirit of unity is what God uses to command the blessing. (See Psalm 133.) We have to make sure that everybody gets in the rhythm to experience this unity and this glory, for when we come together in unity, the anointing is there. When all the people—not just a few people—worship Him, when He can finally get us to come together to sing and praise, we will be of one accord, and His glory will be revealed.

Nobody should be looking on as a spectator; everyone should be participating. I know you may not feel like it, but you're not in the tabernacle of Moses anymore. I know your flesh may be tired, but this is the place where the glory of God takes priority over everything and everybody. God's glory takes precedence over our feelings. It doesn't matter how we feel; He deserves the glory. It doesn't matter what we're going through; He deserves the glory. It doesn't matter what difficulties we've been under; He deserves the glory.

As we sing and shout His praises, blessings come down. The time has come to reach up and let God's deliverance fill the house of the Lord. As we shout, the enemy is driven out. As we shout, God's glory is revealed. God is in our midst. When we shout, we create a wall around the people who are in God's house that the enemy cannot penetrate.

This is Solomon's temple; be mature, and pray the Word of God. If you persevere in worshiping Him, God is going to break loose and heal. He is going to triumph. The King of Glory will be present, and He will command the blessing. He will say, "Live." He will say, "Be healed." He will say, "Be set free."

> *There is a river whose streams shall make glad the city of God, the holy place of the tabernacle of the Most High. God is in the midst of her, she shall not be moved; God shall help her, just at the break of dawn.* (Psalm 46:4–5)

"There is a river whose streams shall make glad the city of God" (v. 4). If you are in the river, you will be glad. God has you in the river, where He wants you; don't leave the river. Dance if He tells you to dance. Let Him bless you in any way He wants. Let Him use anyone He wishes.

I'm thankful for people who are so disciplined, so mature, that they're willing to give God the glory down to the last drop. Remember that the last drop is just as good as the first—maybe even better. God has us in the river now. He's not going to let us go.

Give God glory down to the last drop.

We need to stay in the river; we need to worship Him; we need to sing songs to Him. We need to experience His glory together!

Let's share this prayer as we close this section of the book on worship: May the grace of our God, the keeping power of His Word, and the communing power of His Spirit attend us and saturate us as we commune with Him.

And may we go forth together with joy in the name of Jesus, carrying God's love to others, realizing that we have been...

Part IV
...Loosed for Purpose

Part IV:
Loosed for Purpose

An Overflow of Divine Life

When I was loosed to love, I began to desire a deeper relationship with the Lord so that I could know Him intimately. I embarked on a pathway to intimacy in which I sought Him with all my heart through adoration and worship, and through this I found the love relationship with Jesus that I sought.

However, once I was enjoying and thriving in this intimate relationship with Him, I found that it made me open and available for Him to pour His purposes into me. In this way, the pathway that led to intimacy, the pathway of true and genuine worship, also became the pathway to my discovering and entering into the purposes of the Lord. The two roads of intimacy and purpose share the same path. Having the mind and heart of God, and doing the very will of our Father in heaven, are reflections of the oneness of our relationship with Him. Discovering and living in His purposes is not only personally fulfilling, but also it strengthens our unity in God through His Spirit.

And so, when we worship Christ as Prophet, Priest, and King, we are ready to go out from the presence of the Lord with purpose. As we continually live a life of worship, we find that God saturates us with His Spirit, and an overflow of divine life and purpose pours out from us into the lives of others.

God's purposes are always tied to loving Him and loving those for whom He died. In this way, we come full circle, for this is why we were loosed to love in the first place:

> *"You shall love the* LORD *your God with all your heart, with all your soul, and with all your mind." This is the first and great commandment. And the second is like it: "You shall love your neighbor as yourself."* (Matthew 22:37–39)

Follow the path to intimacy with Christ, and when it comes to God's purpose for you, you'll...

...Walk Right into It

Chapter Ten

Walk Right into It

Entering and maintaining an intimate relationship with Jesus is really the beginning, for God has not finished speaking His ways to us. The question, then, arises, "Where do we go from here?" The answer is that if we will keep pursuing Him and all He has for us, if we will keep loving Him with all our hearts, we are going to walk right into His wonderful purposes, both for us and for those He calls us to serve in love.

It is my privilege to tell you that the Lover of your soul has all kinds of good things waiting for you, and He has placed them all along a pathway to intimacy that is yours and His alone. God has work for you to do, and He will reveal His plan and purpose for your life as you journey with Him on the pathway He reveals. If you understand that you have been loosed to love the Lover of your soul, and if you will commit to following His pathway, you will walk right into all that He has ordained for you. What a glorious revelation of the spiritual rest God has for us as His people!

Maximize Your Moments

At the beginning of this new century and millenium, God's desire is that His people seize every opportunity and maximize every moment, but that they do it while resting in Him. Unfortunately, He sees many of us rushing about doing this and that, feeling pressured to perform or produce. Even when it comes to seizing the moment, for many, the tendency is to try to *make* the moment rather than just to *maximize* it. God doesn't want you to have any stress, because you're too blessed to be stressed. He doesn't want you to feel the pressure of performing. You don't have to perform, because you are already pleasing the only One who counts when you love Him with all of your heart. Hallelujah!

You're too blessed to be stressed.

Often we feel we have to perform for others, to live up to their expectations. Proverbs 16:7 says, *"When a man's ways please the LORD, He makes even his enemies to be at peace with him."* People may not like you, but they will leave you alone just because God will keep them from bothering you. And He'll do it because He knows you love Him. If you are pleasing Him, you won't have to be concerned with trying to please men anymore.

Seek Him with All Your Heart

To know what pleases Him, we must be willing to seek, or pursue, Him. Jeremiah 29:13 tells us how to be successful in our pursuit: *"And you will seek Me and find Me, when you search for Me with all your heart."* God wants us to seek Him with all our hearts, because then, and only then, will we find Him. Exodus 34:14 and Isaiah 48:11 remind us that God is a jealous God and will not share His glory with another. He wants all our love and affection so that He can perfect them and make them the kind of love and affection that will be effective in accomplishing what He has called us to do.

Each of us is Christ's bride. We have been given the privilege of coming into His family so that we can know

Him intimately, and so that He might overshadow us by His Spirit, penetrate us, and give us His seed, which will cause us to bring forth sons into His kingdom. He has not loosed us just so that we can be happy. He has loosed us so that we might be fruitful and multiply after our kind, that we might replenish the earth, subdue it, and take dominion!

Have Patience

Our God challenges us to walk right into all He has for us. In the book of Ruth, there is a very short story about a man and a woman who are connected through divine providence. Allow me to walk you through it. The story opens as a man by the name of Elimelech, who is part of the Israelite family, goes from a safe haven in Bethlehem, of Judah, down to a place called Moab, because there was famine in Judah.

> *Now it came to pass, in the days when the judges ruled, that there was a famine in the land. And a certain man of Bethlehem, Judah, went to dwell in the country of Moab, he and his wife and his two sons. The name of the man was Elimelech, the name of his wife was Naomi, and the names of his two sons were Mahlon and Chilion; Ephrathites of Bethlehem, Judah. And they went to the country of Moab and remained there.* (Ruth 1:1–2)

Elimelech made a permanent decision based upon a temporary situation. Please don't make that mistake. No matter what your current situation may be, count the cost, weigh all the options, and consider the possible long-term effects before making decisions that may have a domino effect on someone else.

Know this: When it comes to seizing the moment and getting all that God has for you, you're going to have to wait patiently on the Lord and be of good courage! He doesn't always come when you want Him to, but He is always on time. Things don't always look good, but His timing is not like ours. We want everything now, but He takes us through a process of growth. If He always gave us what we wanted, when we wanted it, we probably wouldn't know what to do with it when we got it. We couldn't handle it if it were given to us too soon. Can you identify with this truth? Is there anything you honestly can say that you are glad God withheld? I thought so.

Walk in God's Pathway

Instead of giving us all that we want, exactly when we want it, God leads us on His pathway of getting to know Him; I like to call this pathway the pathway to intimacy. God carries us through a process of preparation, so that when we finally get what He has for us, He knows we can handle it. Like a good father, God is not going to give us the keys to the car if He knows He can't trust us to drive it where He says to drive it. He prepares us for His blessings, because His blessings are already prepared for us. They are waiting to overtake us and run us down!

On the pathway to intimacy, as we allow Him to see into us to the extent that we don't mind whatever insights or faults He reveals to us, He will shine the light of His Word into our hearts, clean out the cobwebs, and move us to another level. Even if it hurts, that's okay, because we are sure that He's ultimately working for our good. Even if He has to cut us, we know that He is able to cut with such precision that He will not castrate us. He will not destroy us. He will take out what needs to be taken out, put in what we don't even have sense enough to ask Him for, and sew us back up so well that no one will ever see the scar. That's the kind of Master Surgeon we have. Our heavenly Father loves us so much that He is willing to operate on us individually, according to our particular nature and needs. In addition, He doesn't expose us to others while we're on the operating table. He will do His work in His secret place—in private. In other words, we will have private struggles, but public victories! That's the kind of God we serve. He knows us like no other, and He wants us to know Him and give Him the same love in return.

When we come into His presence, we should tell Him, "Lord, I want to know You; I want to know You better than I know myself. Then, Lord, I want You to show me myself, so that I can see everything that You are fixing. I want to know everything You're putting in and everything You're taking out, so that I will appreciate the work that You are doing on me, in me, and through me. And Lord, when You're finished taking me, blessing me, breaking me, molding me, and making me, I don't mind if You put me in the oven and bake me through and through, because I know that You're making me into something good. Now, when I come out, I'm coming out both palatable and nourishing, and somebody is going to be able to taste and see by my life that the Lord is good!" To use another analogy, we're being fired in the oven of God's love so that all our impurities will be taken away, and we will come out as pure gold. In this, God will be glorified!

> We will have private struggles, but public victories.

This is the kind of mind-set God wants us to have. And when we have it, we won't try to rush or manipulate Him. We will understand that we're in this for the long haul. Talk to yourself and say, "I really don't have to rush this thing. I can take my time and rest. I can walk with Him, and just talk with Him, and let Him take me on the pathway from one degree of grace to another: from faith to faith, from strength to strength, and from glory to glory."

Now, we don't completely change overnight. Remember, "nobody lies down a blunder and wakes up a wonder" in the kingdom of God. All of us have to go through a process; all of us have to go through testings and trials in order to come out with a testimony. But when God brings you through, it is so that He can take you into your inheritance and His purpose.

As I wrote earlier, God has work for you to do, and He will reveal His plan and purpose for your life as you journey with Him on the pathway He reveals. He hasn't saved you so that you can sit on your blessed assurance and wait until Jesus comes for you. He has saved you and set you apart—sanctified you—as holy for Himself and His purpose.

Keep to the Covenant

Let us keep this in mind as we move forward with our story from the book of Ruth. Elimelech goes down to Moab, in the midst of the famine, and he takes his whole family down with him, thereby creating a family crisis. When the priest of the house, who is in covenant relationship with God, moves in disobedience or a lack of faith, the whole family loses the benefits of the covenant and suffers. Elimelech did it, and, unknowingly, as the priest of the house, many other men have done it as well. Some have left God's will and taken their whole families into bondage because they were not hearing and trusting God. Sometimes they have left because of a money shortage, a little lack of food in the land, or other challenges. This man leaves a place of blessing and praise, and goes down to Moab.

God will test our faith, and refine or strengthen it, just to make sure that we don't make a permanent wrong decision in the midst of a temporary crisis. You don't ever have to decide something right away that could change your life forever, just because things are not going well today. Critical decisions in life don't have to be rushed. Sit on the situation a while. Pray, give it to God, and rest. He will work it out. Be still and know that He is God (Psalm 46:10). *"Stand still, and see the salvation of the LORD"* (Exodus 14:13). Tell yourself, "No hurry, no worry, God is in control." He's the One who's leading. He has His easy yoke around your neck. He knows the way, because He is the big ox. We're just the little oxen, going along for the ride.

Setback—or Opportunity?

But Elimelech goes down to Moab. Now, in one place, the Bible calls Moab the *"washpot"* of God (Psalm 60:8). We might interpret this today as the "trash can" of God. Elimelech goes down to a place where there is nothing but trash; he takes his whole family down with him, and shortly after leaving the blessed place of God, he dies and his sons die. The women of the family (his wife, Naomi, and daughters-in-law, Ruth and Orpah) are left in a situation where they are not covered; they have no protection, they have no provision, and seemingly, they have no purpose. They are left in what appears to be a no-win, no-way-out situation. (See Ruth 1:3–5.)

But Naomi is one who has known her God for years, and she is not satisfied with the legacy left by her husband. She knows she can have something better than she has. There are many people today who are sitting in Naomi's seat—perhaps even you are. These people are struggling to overcome less than profitable legacies that have been left to them. Some people have been left bereft of substance because of mistakes they have made. Some are suffering because of mistakes others have made. However, many, like Naomi, have refused to take their setbacks as the last word concerning them. On the contrary, like Naomi, they have realized that they don't have to stay in Moab any longer, because they have been loosed. Their minds have been loosed, and their spirits have been rejuvenated. Their testimonies sound like Naomi's, who said, "I know I went out full, and I might seem like I'm coming back empty, but I'm coming back." (See Ruth 1:21.) These people say, "I may not have the car I had; the divorce took the house; the children may not be able to attend private school any longer, but I'm coming back. I'm coming back to the place of prepared blessings!" Is that your testimony? You, too, can come back to get your bread, no matter what your life has dealt you.

I urge you to say, with Naomi, "I'm going back where I can find some bread, because I hear that God is visiting His people with His Word. I'm going to press my way, and when I get to that place of blessing, I'm going to get some bread (the Word of God)."

> Then [Naomi] *arose with her daughters-in-law that she might return from the country of Moab, for she had heard in the country of Moab that the LORD had visited His people by giving them bread.* (Ruth 1:6)

Naomi was right. God was visiting His people then, and He is visiting His people today with fresh bread and a refreshing from His presence.

A Divine Setup

Through the eyes of faith, Naomi understood that her setback was really a divine setup. Elimelech had made a wrong decision in the midst of a crisis. Naomi, however, made a decision of destiny in the midst of a divine dilemma. This decision affected her and countless others for good, and it fit right into God's plan for the redemption of the world.

Be Careful What You Say

However, even though Naomi recognized that her God was visiting His people back in her homeland, she encouraged her daughters-in-law to go back to their own land instead of going with her. Now, you have to be careful what you say when you're going through a crisis, because somebody is listening to you. You have to be careful what you let come out of your mouth, because somebody is emulating you; somebody who admires you might take what you say and act on it. Naomi gave the wrong kind of testimony, and Orpah listened to her mother-in-law and went back to Moab. She went back to the land of carnality, and she was never heard from again.

Make a decision of destiny in the midst of a divine dilemma.

> *Therefore she went out from the place where she was, and her two daughters-in-law with her; and they went on the way to return to the land of Judah. And Naomi said to her two daughters-in-law, "Go, return each to her mother's house. The LORD deal kindly with you, as you have dealt with the dead and with me. The LORD grant that you may find rest, each in the house of her husband." Then she kissed them, and they lifted up their voices and wept. And they said to her, "Surely we will return with you to your people." But Naomi said, "Turn back, my daughters; why will you go with me? Are there still sons in my womb, that they may be your husbands? Turn back, my daughters, go; for I am too old to*

175

have a husband. If I should say I have hope, if I should have a husband tonight and should also bear sons, would you wait for them till they were grown? Would you restrain yourselves from having husbands? No, my daughters; for it grieves me very much for your sakes that the hand of the LORD has gone out against me!" Then they lifted up their voices and wept again; and Orpah kissed her mother-in-law, but Ruth clung to her. (Ruth 1:7–14)

Today, God is calling us to make the divine decision to leave the land of carnality once and for all. We have been called to leave the land of doing just enough to get by. We have been summoned from the land of mediocrity into a land of excellence where the bread is flowing, where we're moving permanently *"out of darkness into His marvelous light"* (1 Peter 2:9). We must come to a place where we are determined that we are not going back to Moab!

I understand the tendency to go back to what we used to do because it felt good to some degree. Sin does have its pleasure for a season (Hebrews 11:25 KJV). But once you really have been changed and have experienced the presence of God, you will not be able to live in Moab any longer. Sometimes, when you come into the presence of God's people, and they are anointed, you get to the place where you don't like what you're doing. You don't want to stay in what you're doing, and you become sick and tired of being in a pigpen of a lifestyle. You are ready to leave Moab for good!

God Will Use You to Bring Others Out

I'm sure you understand that not everybody who is in the pigpen is happy there. However, at times, it will take somebody else to pull these people out, because they don't realize that they can get out. That's why, once

God has loosed you, He is going to send you back to the pigpen on a rescue operation. There are some folks who are stuck in your former pigpen, and who are waiting for you to come back and tell them, "You don't have to sleep with Larry anymore," or "You don't have to run around with Rosita behind your wife's back." You can tell them that God has something better for them on His pathway to intimacy, and God will use you to pull them out. Look at what God did through Naomi. In spite of the momentary lapse in her witness, at some point Naomi had been strong in talking about her God. Ruth had been listening. Through Naomi's early witness—and a life to back it up—Ruth had seen enough to draw her onto the pathway.

Orpah, on the other hand, was listening also, but she caught only the part where Naomi said that she could go back, because she really wanted to go back anyway. Beloved, you are going to tell some folks that there is a way out, if they want it, but they are not going to come out. They don't want to come out, and they are not going to let you pull them out. So don't continue to waste your time on them. If they don't want to hear you, and you have done what the Lord told you to do, kick the dust off your feet (see Matthew 10:14) and tell them it is their choice, even if they choose hell. Just let them know in parting that there is a way out!

You Can't Go Back!

Oh, but Ruth was sick and tired of the pigpen. I can imagine her saying to Naomi, "I know Moab, and I'm sick and tired of carnality. I'm sick and tired of acting like I'm saved. I really want to be saved and live a life of true faith. I don't want to just talk the life; I want to be able to walk this thing out. I want to live right. So I'm not staying in

Moab. You can't make me go back, and I will not leave you. Don't even ask me to."

> *Ruth clung to her. And [Naomi] said, "Look, your sister-in-law has gone back to her people and to her gods; return after your sister-in-law." But Ruth said: "Entreat me not to leave you, or to turn back from following after you; for wherever you go, I will go; and wherever you lodge, I will lodge; your people shall be my people, and your God, my God. Where you die, I will die, and there will I be buried. The LORD do so to me, and more also, if anything but death parts you and me."*   (Ruth 1:14–17)

If we were at a meeting where I was speaking this message, this would be the place where I would tell you to look at your neighbor and say, "I can't go back!" In weak moments, you may think you want to go back and visit, and you may visit, but you can't stay, because you've been changed. You can't even cuss like you used to cuss. Because you are a *"new creation"* (2 Corinthians 5:17) in Christ, even if you tried to cuss somebody out, it would probably come out as speaking in tongues. Even if you tried to dance the way you used to in your former lifestyle, it would probably come out as the holy dance every time. Why? Because you are not the same once you move from Moab to Bethlehem-Judah (House of Bread and Land of Praise)!

You may visit, but you can't stay, because you've been changed.

Ruth had cleaved to Naomi's God. She said to Naomi, in effect, "Don't try to make me leave you. I've got to go where you go. I've got to go to your church. I've got to find your God. Your God is my God; your people are my people. I don't have to go back to the club; the people there are not my people. My people are the people of God! I'm willing to die with the people of God!" What a powerful covenant she made with Naomi. Well, I feel just like Ruth. I can say to others, "I don't care if you laugh at me because I go to church every Sunday. Where else am I going to go to get my faith strengthened? I'll go on Monday, and if the church is open on Wednesday, I'll be there." In essence, that is what Ruth said to Naomi.

The story of Ruth teaches us that, when we're in a crisis situation, it's very important for us to wait for God's leading. Then, when we do make a decision, it's important that we always give the kind of witness, the kind of divine dialogue, that allows people to be encouraged about what God has done for us, because destiny is calling somebody's name through our voices. Ruth heard her name called, and so did you. Somebody prayed for you. Somebody witnessed to you. Somebody talked to you. Somebody said something good about God, and you heard it. When the time came, I know you were probably caught up in all kinds of things that didn't honor God. At a certain time in our lives, most of us were in the same situation, but God called us out. At a certain point, God knew it was time for you to come out of that mess, to come out of Moab. So He simply called you by name.

The old saints used to say it like this, "Hush! Hush! Somebody's calling my name!" When He called my name, I had to leave Moab. I had to. I was on the dance floor with Joey, but I had to tell him, "Excuse me, Joe, but I've got to go, because Somebody is calling my name." That's how Ruth felt. "I'm sorry, but I've got to cut it loose, let it go, send it back, mark it 'Return to sender.' I'm going where God is taking me, and I've got to go all the way! Yes, I've got to go all the way. I can't get stuck between Moab and Bethlehem. I've got to keep walking, because I've got to walk right into what God has for me, what He's calling me to!"

Say No to the Flesh

Now, when you learn to walk right and to say no to your flesh, don't compromise with it. You can't negotiate with it, because it will win every time. You have to kill it. When I say kill it, I don't mean stab it to death, but rather starve it. This means that you are not to give in to the suggestions that come from your mind or your body that are contrary to God's Word. Instead, you should feed the spirit-man, because whatever you feed—your flesh or your spirit—will flourish.

You have to tell the flesh no, and mean no. You have to be firm and declare: "Shut up, flesh! I'm not doing that." "No, you can't have that." "No, he's married, and I can't have him." "No, she's just like me, and I can't have her, either." No, no, no, and no means *no,* and that's all that it means. Point to yourself, as if pointing to your fleshly nature, and say, "Kill it, kill it, kill it; refuse it; shut it down." That's when God knows you really mean business concerning the flesh. He says, "Ah, now you're walking right." Just take a couple of steps and say, "I'm walking right. And I'm going to walk right into what God has for me!"

You Have a Designed Destiny

When you get to walking right, something happens. You have a designed destiny. A destiny is simply the ultimate destination that God is calling you to. And you don't have anything to do with that. It comes from Him, and not you. God chose a destiny for you. He will reveal it to you more and more. You don't even have the right to look at somebody else and get upset because they are doing something you wanted to do. There's no room for envy or covetousness. God says, "If I wanted you to do it,

I'd let you do it," or "If I knew I could trust you to do it, you would be doing it. You may be doing it after a while, but I can't trust you to do it right now, so I have you doing this instead." Perhaps it just isn't the right time. Be content with whatever state you're in (see Philippians 4:11), and watch Him take you to where He is leading you. Don't get mad at a fellow believer in the Lord because she has the microphone; you don't know how long it took her to get it, you don't know what she had to go through to get it, and you don't know what it's costing her to keep it!

God has a destiny for you, and He will reveal it to you more and more.

Beloved, desire is a very important motivator, and divine desires are given by God. When you have a desire that God has given you, it has come from within the deep cavern of worship. When God sees you worshiping Him, when you seek His face, when you have a visitation with Him, when you go in where He is, let Him talk to you. Stop complaining to Him all the time. Stop always telling Him what's wrong. Go on in, sit on His lap, and say, "Here I am, Daddy. I just came to see You. I just want You to know I'm glad You're my Father. I'm glad You love me. I'm glad to be here. Others have treated me badly, but I'm glad You never did. Thank You for being my Father."

When God sees He's gotten our attention, He pours out His blessings into us. He says, "Oh, I see you are a worshiper. You're delighting yourself in Me. I'm going to give you the desires of your heart, and I'll put what I want you to have inside you. I'll cause you to desire the place I'm getting ready to take you to. I'll cause you to desire the best!"

You don't have to make things up as you go along. Just bless the Lord. Stand still and give Him glory, and

He will pour His desire into your spirit. He'll let you know where He wants you to go and what He wants you to do. When you love Him, you want to please Him, and you say, "Yes, Lord." The result is that desire comes as divine direction.

So Ruth follows Naomi to Bethlehem. She has no money. She is *broke,* but she is not *busted* or *disgusted.* Now, you can be one of the three, but you don't have to be all of them. Being broke is just a temporary shortage of funds. We are able to say, "I'm broke just because the check hasn't come in the mail yet. I'm broke because I'm in between the installments that God is going to give me. Don't even think I'm destitute. Money is coming to me. It just hasn't gotten to me today. But check with me next week. God will bring it to pass. If I need it, it's coming. Now, if I don't need a million dollars, I may not get a million dollars. But if I need it, it will be there, because *'my God shall supply all* [my] *need according to His riches in glory'* (Philippians 4:19)."

And so Ruth says, "I don't have any money, but I have a mind to work. I have a mind to make a difference. There is a desire inside me." And when you have a desire inside you, you don't have to have any money. You have favor and...

...The Secret Ingredient

Chapter Eleven
The Secret Ingredient

W hen we prepare our hearts, when we have the design and the desire to be what God wants us to be, and we seek Him, He doesn't let us come to Him and just sit; instead, He gets us ready to go to work. He gives us a mind to work and a mind to give. That's the mindset that Ruth had.

Love Is the Foundation

The first thing God shows us is that *love* is the underpinning, the foundation, for everything we do. Love is the secret ingredient that makes everything we do prosper. God is calling us to come to Him so that He can show us how to truly love. When you love God with all your heart, mind, soul, and strength, then you can love your neighbor, because God teaches you how to love yourself. Matthew 19:19 says, *"You shall love your neighbor **as** yourself"* (emphasis added). When you come to Him, He teaches you how to love yourself in spite of yourself! He shows you what's bad, He shows you what's good, and He shows you how to love yourself in spite of what's bad and what's good. He gives you His kind of love for yourself. And when He does, He lets you know that He has loosed you so that you can love somebody else with His love.

God has given you love so that you can give it away. When you show God how much you love Him, then He knows He can get love through you to others. And when He starts getting love through you, more love will come back to you. Love begets love, I promise you. It just keeps going; it just works. You can be hateful if you want to, but God says that when you really love people with His love, they'll love you. They'll love you even if they don't understand you. Even if they don't particularly agree with you, they'll love you in return, because love is like a magnet. You can fuss and you can cuss, and people will look at you and ignore you; they'll put their hands on their hips and walk away from you. But it's hard for somebody to argue with you, fuss at you, or hate you while you're showing love to them. They may not like you. They not treat you right. But keep on loving, because love never fails, and you have been loosed to love!

> When you show God how much you love Him, He knows He can get love through you.

How are you going to say you love God when you resent everybody in your church, everybody in the choir, and everybody on the usher board? How can you say you love God whom you have not seen when you hate your brother or your sister whom you see every day? (See 1 John 4:20.) The devil is a liar when he tells us that we can love God without loving our brothers and sisters. God doesn't work like that. He says, "If you really come to Me and you really seek My face, I'm going to give you love, and you're going to be able to look past people's faults." God loves us, and He gives us love for others. *"We know that we have passed from death to life, because we love the brethren"* (1 John 3:14)—not because we speak in tongues, not because we prophesy, but because we have the ability to love the unlovable.

Now, God gives us divine direction as our God-given desire leads us into the field to labor in love. Ruth loved God. She loved Naomi also, and God gave her a mind to work in the fields gleaning food for Naomi and herself. Modern-day Ruths can say, "I'm going to work, because if I don't work, I won't eat. Well, I don't want to sit in the kingdom of God and be a welfare case. I'm not working just for temporal things. I'm also working for a heavenly reward. I'm working to hear Him say, 'Well done!' I'm saved. I'm on my way to heaven. I'm already enjoying the trip. But the work that I'm doing for the kingdom is to hear Him say, 'Well done.'" How about you?

Now, if He's going to say "Well done" to us, we're going to have to do our work well. That means we're going to have to have a mind to work. Point to yourself and say, "Get a job." I don't mean a job at the post office. I mean a job in the kingdom of God.

God Gives the Promotions

God is passing out the job descriptions and the promotions. You don't have to get your job description from your pastor. You don't have to get it from your church leaders. Get the direction for your life from God. When He gives you the vision, and you say, "I'm going to work," then *"whatever your hand finds to do, do it"* (Ecclesiastes 9:10). You have to be faithful over a few things before He can make you a ruler over many. (See Matthew 25:21.) Please God first! Wherever you are right now, be faithful there.

How does this work out in practical terms? Maybe you want a Lexus, but your Volkswagen is dirty, with old French fries and hamburgers from McDonald's scattered throughout it. You can't get anybody to ride in your car because of all the mess. God says, "Clean that car, and

I'll give you another." You want a new house, but you haven't taken care of the one you have. The kitchen is full of dirty dishes! You have roaches, and there are clothes all over the floor. God says, "Clean your house, and I'll give you a new house." You want a husband, but you walk around with your hair in rollers. You don't have any makeup on, and you don't know how to cook. God says, "Get yourself together. If you'll please Me, I'll send you somebody. If you'll look good for Me, I'll make you look good for somebody else. I'll show you off, but you have to please Me."

Use Your Gift

You need to go to work for the Lord now. If you have a song, sing. If they won't let you sing in the choir, sing at nursing homes; sing at hospitals. If you can't sing, you have something else to offer, because all of God's people have been given a gift. I may not be able to sing like the angels, but I can talk like God told me to talk. I may not be able to express myself the way Bishop Jakes does when he says, "Get ready, get ready, get ready!" but I can do what I can do, and nobody else can do what I do. I have a unique gift, and so do you. God says you have to get ready to use your gift, because every gift comes from Him, and He is holding each of us accountable for using the gifts He has given us.

Let me say here briefly that sometimes people will become envious of others' gifts. Nobody has the right to get upset with you because of your gift. And if you have more than one gift, just say to yourself and others, "They're the coat of many colors that my Father gave me. He's responsible for them."

When God endows you, it's because He has a special place where He wants to use what He has given you.

It might not be on a stage before thousands of people, but it might be in the penitentiary in your city. Go into the field and do what your hands find to do.

Now, when you go into the field, God is going to tell others to leave you alone, just as Boaz told the workers not to bother Ruth in the field. (See Ruth 2:8–9.) He will protect you because you worship Him, because you love Him with all your heart. Even when you come in to worship Him, He'll tell others to leave you alone, because you're doing what you can. You've given Him your heart. You've given Him your hands. You're giving Him your best!

> Go into the field and do what your hands find to do.

Give God Your Best

God doesn't want anything but your best. So when you come to Him, you have to be prepared to give Him all that you have. You can't give Him just a small amount, as if you're trying to appease Him, because He knows what you are holding back.

When you come to Him, you have to break open your whole alabaster box of oil. Yes, you do. You have to pour it all out on Him. I do! I tell Him, "I love You; I love You. I love You so much that I want to satisfy You. And I want to satisfy You so much that I'll set the mood. I'll turn off the lights and turn on the praise music. Then I'll light a candle and wait for You to come. And once I set the mood, I'll fluff the pillows of my mind and get my head in the right place so I can receive what You have, and give You what I have. Hallelujah! And when I feel You starting to penetrate me and take me where I've never been before, I'll tell you that 'any way You bless me, Lord, I'll be satisfied.' I'm going to pour it all on You, because You're my Husband. Others won't understand this, but I've got to give You the praise and the glory and the worth that is due You. If I look silly, I won't mind, because You will defend me."

As you give God your best, the enemy will try to mock you, but Jesus will make him leave you alone. As you worship, somebody might be rolling his eyes, but God will convict him right where he sits. He gives you divine protection, so why not give Him all you have? He'll protect you! Like Ruth, spiritually speaking, He won't let the workers hurt you. He won't let them rape you. He'll put you in a field. He'll place you in a position under divine leadership. He won't allow you to be a "Lone Ranger" Christian. He will plant you in the house of the Lord under His protection—under the leader of His choice, His Boaz. He will give you a mighty leader who will provide protection and covering for you. And God will use people to leave you...

...Handfuls of Purpose

Chapter Twelve
Handfuls of Purpose

Just as Boaz protected and provided for Ruth, God will protect and provide for His children. Boaz told the workers to let handfuls of grain fall to the ground on purpose so that Ruth could glean them. (See Ruth 2:15–16.) The King James Version says that Boaz asked his workers to let *"handfuls of purpose"* fall for Ruth. Similarly, God will tell people to leave handfuls of purpose for you. He will purposely leave things for you to do. While you are "gleaning," you are going to be walking into blessings, because you are going to be in the divine place of God. So don't leave the field you're in. If God has put you there, you'd better stay. You need to be planted. It doesn't matter if you're not in the limelight. You need to shine where you are. And you would be wise to wait until the sunlight comes upon you before you try to shine. You can't make the moment, but when it comes, and the light is shining on you, you should maximize it and say, "Here I am, God. You know You can trust me. I knew You would give me the opportunity sooner or later." And when it comes, acknowledge that God has brought you there, and do what He has told you to do. Again, be faithful where you are.

If you're not allowed to preach, it's because God knows you're not ready to preach. He can't even trust you to come to Sunday school. How is He going to let you preach? You don't want to go to Bible study, and you don't want to go to prayer, so how are you going to lead somebody where you yourself don't go? God says, "I'll get you ready first. I'll give you a few things to get you gleaning in the field."

You may be cleaning the carpet right now. You may be a Sunday school teacher right now. When God gets ready to act on your divine purpose, He takes you one step at a time, because that's all you can handle. Remember to be faithful over the few things He gives you to do at first. God places into your hand handfuls of divine purpose and then enables you to grow into greater things.

When God acts on your divine purpose, He takes you one step at a time.

Do What You Can; Use What You Have

It may take a long time of preparation, but don't worry. Let me give you an example from my own life. I was a Sunday school teacher as a teenager. Sometimes I taught two people, and sometimes I taught twenty. And when it came to the point where God knew I could handle more than twenty, He let the state Sunday school superintendent say, "Would you come and teach in our Sunday school convention?" And I thought to myself, "This must be God's purpose." Well, I spent a whole year getting ready. I spent a whole year getting ready to teach for one hour at a Sunday school convention. When the time came, and I taught, the Lord blessed. A man sitting in the back said, "Oh, by the way, would you come to my church and preach on the letter M for Mother's Day?"

Now, some folks are too proud to preach on M. They say, "I don't want to preach on M. I'm a preacher; let me preach on the whole word *Mother,* or don't give me anything at all." God says to such people, "You aren't going to get anything at all, because you're not even willing to take M." Beloved, you have to be willing to start where God puts you. Do what you can, use what you have, and watch God walk you from one degree of purpose into another.

When I was asked to preach on the letter M, I said, "Well, God must know I can only handle M." I went home and I started to study M. I turned M every way I could. I turned it upside down, and I turned it inside out. By the time I got through with M and preached the message, the man said, "Can you come back next year and preach on O-T-H-E-R? I said to myself, "Purpose." That was another handful of purpose from God. So I went and preached on the rest of the word, and God blessed it.

Then many invitations started coming. So "over the river and through the woods to Grandmother's house I went" in a little Volkswagen. Sometimes I went on the train or on the bus. Those who invited me would send me a ticket. I didn't have an entourage; I didn't have anybody to carry my bag. I didn't even have a bag—I just had a Bible; I just had a word from the Lord. I went where I could go. I didn't ask for a first-class ticket. I didn't ask for a hotel room. I went and stayed with the saints. I slept on the saints' floors and ate the saints' food. It was holy food, sanctified food. And when I preached, I didn't care if I preached to only twenty people, because I wasn't preaching for them; I was preaching for Him, and I knew He was listening.

And so I would preach for twenty people. The congregation would give me twenty-five dollars, and I'd say, "Thank You, Lord. Now I can buy gas for my car." *Purpose.*

Now, in God's own time, when He knew I was ready, He allowed a mighty spiritual warrior to call me and say, "Would you come and preach in my church?" I said, "I'd be glad to." I didn't ask how many members he had or how much money he was going to give me, because I trusted God to provide for me and the people. All I knew was that God has said, *"Freely you have received, freely give"* (Matthew 10:8). For God's sake, I was ready to go. I went on the plane to West Virginia, and I preached for a few wonderful people. We prayed, laid hands on those who needed prayer, and rolled around in the flow of the Spirit; we had a good time with that. A little while later, I went back to preach for this same pastor, and I didn't have to stay in his apartment with his family. I stayed in a hotel and ordered room service. I thought, *"Purpose."* All this time, I kept traveling around the country as an evangelist, holding meetings. I stayed at the Motel 6; then I moved up to the Super 8, each stop being filled with God's purpose!

Later on, this same pastor from West Virginia called back and said, "Would you facilitate for me?" I didn't know what *facilitate* meant; I had to look it up. If you don't know something, you'd better ask somebody. You have to know what you're doing. You have to know what God is calling you to do before you can do it effectively.

God is not calling us just for destiny; He's calling us for legacy. He is calling us to contribute, to leave some-thing behind, beloved. But He is not just calling for legacy. He is also calling for accuracy. He wants us to get it right. We don't have time to trip over things anymore. We don't have time to miss God anymore. We have to get rid of anything that would hinder our journey. So I said, "God, what is *facilitate*?" He said, "It doesn't mean preaching." So I

God is calling us for destiny, legacy, and accuracy.

looked it up, and it meant to keep things going, to keep the service moving at a reasonable pace.

Now, the man who had asked me to facilitate sent me a first-class ticket to California. I got on an airplane and went from one airport to another airport without touching down. I thought, "I have never been on an airplane that stayed up in the air this long," but I knew it was *purrpose.* I got off the airplane, and there was a limousine driver holding up my name on a card. I hadn't ever been in a stretch limousine in my life, much less by myself, but the card had my name on it. I thought, *"Purrrpose."* I was driven to the hotel. Beloved, it wasn't a Motel 6; this hotel was way up in the air. I was directed to the top suite, and I walked into a room that was as big as my house. It had fruit baskets and everything. I said, *"Purrrrpose."* When God promotes us, it is for His purpose, but it sure blesses us!

Then the limousine driver came for me again and took me over to the convention center. I went up on stage, and a precious man, whose name is David, handed me a microphone. It was the first time I had seen a microphone that didn't have a cord on it. And I said, "Is that my mike? Look at that mike; I have never seen a mike like that." He said, "Say something," and I said, "What?" He said, "Give me a sound check." I said, "What's a sound check?" He said, "Just say anything," and I said, "Hallelujah." You have to know what to say when you get the microphone, beloved. You have to know who made it possible for you to have the microphone. Glory to God! David said, "That will work fine." Then I was driven back to the hotel.

At 6:30, I was brought back to the convention center. I was directed to walk down a long corridor and knock on a door that had a star on it. A voice said, "Come in." I said, "Is that you, Bishop? Then Bishop T. D. Jakes said,

"Welcome to the kingdom of God and 'Woman, Thou Art Loosed.'" I thought, *"Purrrrrpose!"* He said, "This is what I want you to do, Rita. I want you to take the stage at 7:00 and lead the people in praise. Then I want you to do the announcements. After that, I want you to hand the mike to the psalmist, and when she hands it back to you, hand it to me at 7:30."

You Can Do What God Calls You to Do

I thought, "I can do this!" God never gives you something to do that you can't do. Tell yourself, right now, "I can do this! I can do this! What-ever God gives me to do, I can do." Hear what I say: When God calls me to do something, I don't have to worry; I don't have to apologize; I don't have to retreat. When He calls my name, I'm the woman for the job. I can do this. I may not be able to do *that,* but I can do *this.*

> God never gives you something to do that you can't do.

So I said, "All right," and I went back to the stage. At five minutes to seven, I prayed, "Lord, if You don't help me to do this, it isn't going to be done." Frankly, at that moment, I felt as if I needed Depends; yes, I did. Even today, when I preach, I often feel that way. Although you are to trust God to enable you to do what He's calling you to do, if you ever stop being dependant on Him, and if you ever start thinking you can do it by yourself, you're in trouble. But as long as you say, "God, unless You are doing this, it is not going to be done," you'll be all right. My heart's cry was, "Use me, Lord."

I went out on the stage at 7:00 and stood in front of the podium, facing twenty thousand women. *Twenty thousand women.* My breath went away. But I thought, "Purpose. Purpose." Then I said to the women, "I came all the way from the nation's capital to the City of Angels to ask one question: 'Is there praise in the house for the Lord Jesus Christ?'" and they shouted, "YEAH!" I led them in praise, did the announcements, gave the microphone to the psalmist, and then got it back. It was 7:30. So I said, "And now, mighty women of God, we want to welcome to the stage Bishop T. D. Jaaa-kes!"

Do Only Your Assignment

You have to do what you're told to do. When your pastor asks you to pray over the offering, don't pray over China. Don't pray over Russia. Don't pray over the children in Afghanistan. Just pray over the offering and then sit down. Then when you are called up the next time, do what you're given an opportunity to do. Again, do what you're told. Do your assignment, and then rest in the Lord and sit down. Don't try to do more before God tells you to. When I handed the Bishop the microphone, God blessed. After that, I traveled all over the country to facilitate at his conferences. At the same time, I continued traveling around the country as an evangelist.

Take careful note of this secret to maximizing your moment: When the moment comes, do what you're told, and then be watchful and prayerful. Be careful, because the enemy will try to abort you. People started coming to me and saying, "You know, why doesn't he let you preach? You facilitate, you're the praise lady, but why doesn't he let you preach? You can preach; I bet you can preach; I see the anointing on you." Beloved, that was about five or six years ago, and it wasn't yet my time. I knew it, and God knew it. *Purpose* has to be so established in us that we won't let anybody tell us to do anything God didn't tell us to do. Don't let anybody push you into the forefront when God isn't with you. I told them, "I'm not called a preacher today; I'm called a facilitator! Go look it up!"

Now, when God got ready, and when He knew that He had gotten me ready, the Bishop said, "Would you fill in for my wife and preach?" And I said, "Yes, sir." So I preached, and the Lord blessed. The next week, was I asked to preach? No. I was back to facilitating, and I was back to hitting the road as a traveling evangelist. Nobody knew me as a "celebrity," and I didn't know anyone, either. I was just giving out the Gospel.

But then, years later, the Bishop called and said, "Can you come to Dallas?" I said, "Oh, yes, Bishop, I can come to Dallas any time you say." He repeated, "No, come to Dallas." I said, "Oh, yes, Bishop, just call for me." Then he said, "No, I want you to *move* to Dallas to work at the Potter's House."

On the Launching Pad

All this time, I had been saying, *"Purrrrrpose."* But now, all of a sudden, I found myself saying, "God, is this You?" I really had to pray hard, because I felt as if I were already on a runway, getting ready to take off. I was getting invitations from all over the country, several years ahead. People kept asking, "Will you come preach for us? Will you come preach for us?" I said, "God, I'm on the runway, getting ready to take off, and now you want me to go down and work at the Potter's House? I feel as if You are calling me back to the airplane hangar." God answered immediately, and said, "I'm not calling you off the runway to put you back into the hangar. I'm calling you off the runway to put you onto the launching pad. You have to trust Me when you cannot

> Trust Him when you can't trace Him.

trace Me. You have to trust Me when you don't see how I'm going to do it." So I said, *"Purpose,"* and I went down to the Potter's House. I came off the road to serve Him and the church. I had to tell people no when they asked me to do a preaching engagement. Why? I had gotten a different assignment, and it's all about *purpose.* Now I oversee the training of all in-house ministers at the Potter's House who will one day be presented for licensing and ordination, about 300 students, with a new class getting ready to begin next semester. They will stand before the Bishop at some point, so that he can lay his hands on them when he gets ready to send them out into the vineyard.

Meanwhile, as I focused on my handful of purpose, in the midst of teaching and preaching and working and laboring, the Bishop said, "Evangelist, I want you to preach this year at the 'Woman, Thou Art Loosed' conference." *Purrrrrrrrpose!*

A Step-by-Step Process

Beloved, it has been a step-by-step process. I didn't run into it, and you won't, either. You have to walk right into it. Do what God says as you're going, and God will perfect that which concerns you. But you have to love Him with all your heart. And, if you trust Him enough to obey Him, even when you would rather be somewhere else, doing something else, you will walk right into His purposes and stay in the center of His pathway for you. I preach because I love God, His people, and His Word, and because it is His purpose for me—not because I naturally enjoy it, but because God has equipped me to stand before anyone and not be afraid. It is His purposes that are all-important.

201

Today, I'm still on the path. I preached at the conference this year, but next year I may not. It may not be God's purpose for me. You have to take it one day at a time and play it by ear. You have to hear what God is saying and walk right into all that He has for you without looking back. As the Bible says, *"Forgetting those things which are behind, and reaching forth unto those things which are before, [we] press toward the mark for the prize of the high calling of God in Christ Jesus"* (Philippians 3:13–14 KJV). Each day is a new beginning, and handfuls of purpose await us!

The Greatest of These Is Love

I asked God, "Lord, what do You want me to tell Your people?" and He said, "Love. Tell them to love one another!" Then He told me, "Rita, I have put love in you, and that's why people like being around you; that's why they send for you. You love God's people, and you love God's Word, but you love God first." You can't love God's people and not love Him. And you can't love God's people or Him without loving His Word. But when you love all three—God, His Word, and His people—you become an invaluable asset to any ministry.

Wherever you are serving, your God-given overseer needs to know that you are willing to submit to him or her with respect. *"Let the elders that rule well be counted worthy of double honour, especially they who labour in the word and doctrine"* (1 Timothy 5:17). If my overseer says, "Jump," I say, "How high, sir?" If He says, "Go," I say, "How far, sir?" That is what governs me. And because of that, I'm protected by God, and I have favor with the brethren. God is my heavenly Boaz. All my needs are supplied more than enough. As my pastor, the Bishop is my spiritual Boaz, and I celebrate great blessings under his leadership and covering.

With all that continues to unfold in my life, writing this book has been a special part of God's purposes for me, so that I can share with you how to enter into God's purposes for you. I didn't just enter into my present ministry overnight. It was a process for me, and it will be the same for you. But if you'll keep walking *right*, you're going to walk right into it.

It certainly worked for Ruth as she gleaned in Boaz' field under divine protection and found favor with him. Now, along with favor, preparation and timing became two of Ruth's greatest assets as she listened to the voice of her mentor, Naomi. Tenderly she gave Boaz the opportunity to come to her rescue, and he did. She went from gleaning leftovers in the field to being the heiress and owner of the field, with covenant blessings. (See Ruth 2–4.) Our God will do no less for us as we keep walking in His will with a mind to work in His field.

You may stumble, you may trip, and you may even fall, but get back up. Get back on the path, and keep walking in the direction that God has given you. Don't be a renegade by trying to do things in your own strength. When you start walking right into His purposes with love, it's going to overcome a multitude of faults. (See 1 Peter 4:8.) You will find that everything you need will be provided for. Opportunity will keep on knocking, and, sure enough, you'll be in the right place, the place God has for you. Favor will come, and blessing will come. Remember that our times and seasons are in His hands (Psalm 31:15). I am persuaded that no good thing will He withhold from any of us who walk uprightly before Him (Psalm 84:11).

But we have to make sure we...

Keep walking right, and you'll walk right into God's purposes for you.

...Stay on the Pathway

Chapter Thirteen
Stay on the Pathway

One Sunday morning, the Bishop challenged us. He said, "If you want to be in God's perfect will, if you don't want to miss Him, and you want to make a covenant with Him, then just like Ruth gleaning the field, I want you all to come down to the front; I want you to take an envelope, and I want you to plant a special financial seed with Him." Well, I was with him when he said, "Do you want to be in God's purpose?"

I said, "Yes, sir, Bishop."

"Do you want to be a blessing?"

"Yes, sir, Bishop.

"Do you want Him to use you?"

"Yes, sir, Bishop."

"Put a special offering in an envelope."

And I said, "Is that you, God?" Be careful to hear God. The man of God has the mouth of God. And if you believe God for one thing, believe Him even when He speaks things you don't want to hear. Purpose, destiny, and accuracy come as we obey God completely.

I took that special seed, put it in an envelope, and ran back and gave it to him. Since that day, I have experienced a release. I don't have to worry and ask, "Am I in Your will, God? Did You want me to do this?" I know that purpose, destiny, and accuracy are attending my way. He has loosed me from my fear of people and what they think, with their jealousies and their rolling eyes. He has loosed me to love them and give them what He has given to me. I know He'll do the same for you, because He doesn't love me any more than He loves you.

Some of you are already on track, headed to what God has for you. My conscious prayer for you is that you will keep walking right. Stay under your spiritual leadership, your covering and protection, and submit. Don't let anyone get you off track. You've got too much to gain. You've come too far now. You're going to conceive and give birth in the kingdom to all that God has for you, just as Ruth did! In fact, giving birth to covenant blessings was fulfilled in a literal way in Ruth's life. She was given the tremendous blessing of being the great-grandmother of King David, through whom Jesus the Messiah was descended, the *"mediator of the new covenant"* (Hebrews 12:24).

Maybe you've been nervous or afraid in the past. Remember that God has everything under control. Your times and seasons are in His hands. You don't have to rush or press or be stressed. You just have to keep walking right, and you're going to walk right into it.

How to Stay on the Pathway

I want to conclude with some principles I've discovered for staying on the pathway, because maintaining our relationship with Christ on the pathway to intimacy is not the same as starting it. As I have continued on the path, there are some things that I've done to help me stay on the path, and I'd like to share them with you.

Maintaining a relationship with Christ is not the same as starting it.

208

First let me say that staying on the pathway and walking right is not an overnight, onetime accomplishment. It is a journey, and there will be road signs along the way to ensure that we don't get lost. Even though we might take detours and leave the pathway temporarily, our God will provide enough signs to guide us safely back on course, and to lead us to our preordained destination. Here are some of the signs that have helped me to stay on or, in some cases, to get back on His pathway for my life:

1. Be sure you have really believed on and received Christ. (See 1 John 5:10–13.) The Word of God assures us that our inner man is changed once we receive Christ, and that our hearts are no longer comfortable living a life of sin. (See 2 Corinthians 5:17 and 1 John 3:9.) However, because we are not perfect, we need the assurance that we are children of God, and that nothing can separate us from His love. (See Romans 8:38–39.)

2. Giving God true worship will help you to walk right. (See John 4:23–24 and Psalm 16:11.) I have found that it is extremely difficult to walk according to the dictates of the flesh while I am worshiping. In everyday terms, I have no desire to lust after someone else because I am praising and thanking and loving God. I don't thirst for the finest in wines or liquors, because I'm drinking the new wine of His presence, which creates a high without a hangover! I could go on, but I believe you get the point. Plainly stated, worship will keep you from conforming to the world, while the world, if you let it, will keeping you from worshiping.

3. Study the Word of God, for it lights the pathway of life and shows us His way. (See Psalm 119:105 and Proverbs 3:5–6.) We don't have to be ignorant of what our God wants for us and from us. He says it very plainly in

His written Word. God can help us with every step we take if we will check with Him before taking the step. His Word offers direction for any situation we face. First, His Word will show us where we are (like the little dot on the information map that says "You are here"). Then, after helping us to locate ourselves, His Word will speak direction to our hearts if we will diligently seek Him in prayerful study.

4. Make the choice to obey God's Word. (See Joshua 1:7–8.) Obedience is an act of our wills. We have the God-given right and ability to do what He says once we decide to do so. Our hands, feet, mouth, and other members of our bodies will do only what we tell them to do. Walking right is not by chance, but by choice. Once we choose to obey His Word, we will have *"good success"* (Joshua 1:8).

5. Face reality. (See 1 John 1:8–9.) Do not allow yourself to live in a world of fantasy or falsehood. See and say things as they really are, even when they are not pretty or desirable. Be honest with yourself and with Him, because walking in truth frees us from self-condemnation and the condemnation of others. This allows us to walk in the liberty of God's love and Jesus' sacrifice for us, which is that *"while we were yet sinners, Christ died for us"* (Romans 5:8 KJV). Knowing and acknowledging that Christ died for us frees us from the guilt and penalty of sin. As we face the truth about our sin, and accept His death as payment for it, our hearts cannot help but be filled with love and gratitude that will inspire us to walk right and please Him more and more each day.

6. How to handle detours: If at first you don't succeed, cry and try again! All of us will miss the mark at some point and end up off the path on a detour. I use the word

detour because we leave God's path of righteousness and go "touring" on our own paths. Often, this detour deters us and temporarily derails us from the direction of our destiny. But don't worry, because even on our detours, there will be plenty of God-given signs, strategically placed, to help us locate where we are, determine how we got off track, and find our way back to the right path. All we have to do is *cry out* to God in repentance, as David did in Psalm 51. God will, by His Spirit, speak to our hearts as believers, and lead us back to His righteous path. He also promises to restore lost time to us as we continue on His preplanned course for us. (See Joel 2:25.) What a mighty God we serve!

7. Please the One who really counts. Don't try to please anyone but God, because He is the only One who truly loves you and knows the charted course for your life. Proverbs 16:7 says that if you will concentrate on pleasing the Lord, He will make even your enemies to be at peace with you. Remember that, even if you try, you can't please all of the people all of the time, so just focus on pleasing the only One who really counts, the only One who can get you home! Here are a few things that please Him: faith, worship, humility, obedience, and love for your fellowman.

8. Trust God's silence. Obey what you hear God say, and when He is silent, hold on to the last thing He said until He says something else. This is trust, and trust acknowledges that God knows who you are, where you are, and what you are going through. He has promised never to leave or forsake you (Hebrews 13:5). He may be silent, but He is not absent.

9. Remember that His grace is sufficient. (See 2 Corinthians 12:9–10.) We are saved by grace through faith

(Ephesians 2:8–9), and according to Hebrews 11:6, it is impossible to please God without faith. However, know that you will experience varying degrees of faith on your journey. On some days, you will have the *faith* of the woman with the flow of blood. She pressed her way to touch the grace that was manifested in the hem of Jesus' garment, and she received her healing (Luke 8:43–48). So will you!

On other days, you will have *great faith,* like the woman of Canaan who prayed and worshiped her way into Jesus' heart and received healing for her daughter (Matthew 15:21–28). Likewise, your prayers for the children will touch His grace and be answered.

On still other days, you will have *so great faith,* like the centurion soldier who trusted so strongly in the Word of God that, through his trust, his servant was healed (Luke 7:1–10). Know that, as you trust the Word of God, the power of life and death will be in your mouth as well!

However, there will be days in your life when you will have *little faith,* and you will feel like the widow of Nain. (See Luke 7:11–15.) There will be days when your eyes will be filled with tears and your heart will be broken into a thousand pieces. You will feel as if it is raining and pouring at the same time. You may not feel like praying or singing or seeking God in any way. You may not be able to call up any faith at all. When these days come, and they will, you will discover that they can be the most precious times of all. Why? It will be at those times that you will experience the God of all grace. In your weakness, His strength will be made perfect, or completely known to you, as His love and care come shining through!

If you will look for these signs along the way, I am certain they will help you to stay on His path and keep walking right, even as they continue to help me to this day.

Epilogue

ell, my friend, whatever your station in life is as you near the completion of this book, I encourage you to follow the pathway that has been revealed through this personal portrait of my intimacy with Christ. I had told myself that I wasn't going to share my personal experiences with anybody, but I couldn't keep them to myself! Thus, the pages of this book have been drawn out of me to signal that God loves us with an endless love, and that He changes us so that we might, in turn, be used as agents of change. God doesn't deliver us without purpose. He intends to use us as His willing servants to do His bidding. Finally, beloved, God has loosed all of us to be lovers of Him, ourselves, our families, our neighbors, and everyone else He sends our way.

> God changes us so that we might be used as agents of change.

I must say that I have been forever changed by my encounters with Jesus during our many sessions of "into me see" (intimacy). My heart has become more and more filled with His love. My spirit has become more committed to sharing His love with others than ever before. My mind is free to live. I am free to give of myself, and I am free to receive without reservation, as I rest in His love.

I used to worry about getting old and not being married. Not anymore. Now I just rest in the security of His love as my true, everlasting Husband, and I give Him thanks. I realize that, even if I marry, I'll just be on loan until I get home to Jesus. I am grateful for every gift He gives me. In fact, I thank Him for every day that I am able to see. I thank Him for every birthday I'm able to celebrate, because I've looked at the alternative to getting older, and I don't like it!

I'm so glad to be alive, and what's more, I find absolutely no fault in Him who is the Lover of my soul! When I asked Him, "Where do we go from here?" He said, "From grace to grace, from strength to strength, and from glory to glory!" That means that He and I have only just begun to develop our relationship, and that there is no limit to how close we can be if I'll only stay on the pathway of intimacy.

I've got to stay on that pathway. I've tried detours, and there is just no place as precious as His presence. There is no worldly wealth that can pay for the peace that I feel as I please Him. I have found no greater joy in life than feeling His manifested power through His Holy Spirit as He moves in, around, upon, and through me. What wonderful prepositions to describe His all-inclusiveness in my life!

Beloved, describing the multifaceted effects of loving and being loved by Jesus has been my challenge in writing this book. Why? It is because words fall so short of the glory that comes through an intimate relationship with Him. However, I have sincerely tried to let the abundance of my heart speak, praying that, in some way, no matter where you are in life, you might be inspired and compelled to seek an even deeper level of intimacy with Jesus, who is truly the Lover of your soul.

Epilogue

It is my heart's desire that Jew and Gentile, male and female, people of all races and every age group, would embrace this book and use it as a guide to the pathway of intimacy that has been opened by the blood of Jesus, God's Lamb and our Lover. Walk right into all that God has for you, gathering more and more purpose along the way.

In closing, if you know Jesus as Savior and Lord, read on to get the conclusion of the whole matter. If you have never accepted Jesus Christ as your Savior and Lord, please know that He is truly the Lover of your soul. He died to open a pathway of intimacy for you that leads back to His Father, and He longs to lead you there. Receive Him right now into your heart. Acknowledge Him as the Lover of your soul, and sincerely desire to satisfy Him as such. Tell Him that you want Him more than anyone or anything. Then, set the mood for an intimate exchange by creating an atmosphere of praise and worship for Him to inhabit. Fluff the pillows of your mind to make sure your head is in the right place to receive and give His love.

Jesus died to open a pathway of intimacy to the Father—and He longs to lead you there.

Allow tears of joy or sorrow to water your heart. Let Him know that you trust Him and that you are completely open for Him to penetrate your spirit and saturate you with all of who He is. Then, rest in His love and allow Him to take you where you've never gone before.

Take your time, and make sure that what you are experiencing is real and not the simple fabrication of emotionalism. Finally, in the afterglow of His loving presence, allow Him to sow into your life the reproductive seeds of vision, purpose, invention, and any others He chooses. I promise you that these seeds, born out of intimacy with

217

Him, will germinate and bring forth much fruit that will remain. (See John 15:16.) He will even give you a glimpse of where He is taking you from here. Whatever you do, stay on the path!

My Prayer for You

Lord, thank You so much for allowing me to share our love with this reader. Beloved, I pray that the words of this little book have painted a portrait of intimacy upon the canvas of your heart that will never grow dim. I pray that you will draw closer and closer to the Lover of your soul and find in Him more than you ever knew you could have. Lord, please lead this precious one to Your pathway of intimacy and feed them all along the way. Don't let them go until they realize the true joy and privilege of having been loosed to love. For it is in the sweet name of Jesus, the Lover of my soul, I pray. Amen.

About the Author

Dr. Rita Twiggs has served as an evangelist for over twenty-five years. She is an anointed preacher, teacher, facilitator, seminar and workshop leader, choral director, singer, and author. Dr. Twiggs is currently the Dean of the Potter's House School of Ministry in Dallas, Texas, under the leadership of Bishop T. D. Jakes, Sr. She is also a gifted servant with an unwavering commitment to declare the whole counsel of God. The theme of her life is found in Nehemiah 8:10: *"Then he said unto them, Go your way, eat the fat, and drink the sweet, and send portions unto them for whom nothing is prepared: for this day is holy unto our Lord: neither be ye sorry; for the joy of the LORD is your strength"* (KJV).